Misadventures of a
HAPPY HEART

A Memoir of Life Beyond Disability

AMY F. QUINCY

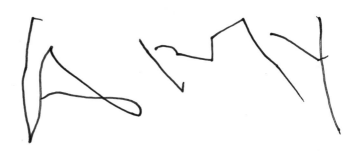

For Mom, with love and gratitude —

there's no one I'd rather take this journey with.

ACKNOWLEDGEMENTS

This entire manuscript was written in a writing workshop led by Carol D. O'Dell, so first and foremost I want to thank her for her leadership and guidance throughout this process. The members of that workshop, the Chat Noir Writers Circle, also deserve my thanks for their critiques, read-throughs, support and friendship; specifically Diane Perrone and Nancy Purcell, who helped me attempt to dot every "i" and cross every "t," as well as take out or add commas (well, in my case, take out). And, of course, I want to thank the many teachers in my life. Early ones who fanned the flames of a dream, and much later, one named Mark Ari, who was the first professional who made me believe I was any good at this crazy endeavor. Thank you.

DISCLAIMERS

My biggest fear in writing this memoir has been that I would write something that would hurt some family member or friend. But I've learned that it is this kind of self-censorship that stifles great writing. So I've tried simply to write my truth. Not *the* truth, but the truth as I see it, which in reality is just an opinion. Names have been changed in some cases and not in others, in a way that probably only makes sense to me. My wish for this book is that it can provide comfort to people going through similar or any life changing events and that it helps close the gap between the able-bodied and disabled worlds so that our shared world becomes that much more inclusive.

TABLE OF CONTENTS

Prologue: October 3, 2006

A CATEGORY 5

Three paramedics arrive. They're all good-looking. I mouth the word "cute" to Lee Anne over their bent heads and raise my eyebrows suggestively. She catches it and smiles. I scan for wedding rings. There's just something about a take-charge, good-in-a-crisis man.

"Can you make it down the stairs?" the strongest-looking blonde asks me. Now that I'm up from my bed and we're all standing outside my apartment, I can see he's too short. Damn.

"Sure," I say. I start to take the first step and my knees buckle. Immediately, there's a paramedic under each arm.

"Guess not," I joke.

I've filled them in. The headache, the nausea, the mass in my head. I even had the MRI film from August to show them. Dr. Campbell had slapped the image of my brain up against the light and laughingly asked if I could see the problem. He was being sarcastic. You didn't need to have graduated med school to know something was wrong. It was the size of a golf ball. A cluster of blood vessels had malformed 36 years ago. They weren't supposed to be there.

I've often been asked if I was scared. Call me naive. I failed to grasp the gravity of my situation. It's true what they say. Nobody believes anything bad will ever happen to them. In my case, I didn't believe it even *while* it was happening.

The closest I came to real fear was that moment on the bathroom floor after I grabbed my cell phone. Twice I had attempted dialing 9-1-1. Twice I heard three unmistakable tones. Misdials. I don't remember my double vision or a lack of motor control starting then. But it was undeniable. There was a problem. Three little numbers. And I couldn't dial them. I was alone in the apartment. Unable to call for help. Fear flashed. Ten seconds, maybe. And then it was gone. There was a knock at the door. My friend, Lee Anne.

I wave goodbye to her through the back ambulance window. She's on my cell phone. She's calling Vivian to meet us at the hospital where Dr. Campbell works.

I feel fine now. The nausea's gone. It's just this headache. Lee Anne offered to bring me her migraine medicine earlier that morning. I had taken her up on it. Thank God. Lee Anne is like that. Maternal. She calmly helped me pick out something to wear while we waited for the ambulance. "Now remember, it's gonna be cold in there," she said. It was still warm, October in Florida, but we decided on a sweatshirt with my shorts.

The ambulance takes a turn. My body shifts on the stretcher, and I readjust the sheet. My right leg doesn't feel the same as my left leg. My left leg feels the cool, thin cotton over me, the hard metal beneath me, the warm skin of my other thigh. My right leg doesn't feel any of that. There's just this tingling, like when your arm falls asleep at night and you have to massage the blood back into it to get it moving. It's like a giant wave washed over me when we turned, sweeping away the sensation. "My right side is going," I announce to the men. "I can feel it. It just went."

Even this is said matter-of-factly, without alarm. So they'll know. After all, I'm heading to the hospital. The staff there will fix everything.

When I arrive in the emergency room, MRI film on my stomach, Vivian appears and begins speaking Nurse with the ladies here. People in uniform swirl around me with equipment. I'm grateful for Viv's presence. She's a friend, but also a professional. Her high-energy, commanding way, which I usually find draining and abrasive in the outside world, is ideal in this environment. Every facet of her personality seems custom-tailored to fit her job in an ER. I'm hooked up to an IV. Lee Anne and Vivian pass the time with me in a little room off to the side, partitioned by a curtain.

It hasn't escaped my attention that Dr. Campbell isn't whisking me off to perform the surgery he so boldly claimed to have done quite often. Instead, he comes in at intervals to conduct little neurological tests which I gather I'm failing. He's in contact with Dr. Diaz in Miami regarding my condition, which seems to be rapidly deteriorating. A mirror image of everything in sight has appeared at some point. I sound drunk and everyone has an identical twin.

"Say 'no ifs, ands, or buts,'" Dr. Campbell instructs.

"No ifs, ands, or buts," I slur.

"Raise your hands like you're holding two pizzas." He flips his palms skyward. The action looks more to me like a waitress carrying two cocktail trays, but I comply. Or try to. My right-hand doesn't lay flat. The fingers are curling up slightly. I laugh it off.

"Well, it's a mangled pizza, but it's a pizza!"

Everyone in the room cracks up.

I feel an anxiousness in recounting these events that I didn't feel at the time. I want to take that girl lying there by the shoulders and shake her. I want to yell at the doctors and nurses, "Somebody do something! What are we all waiting around for? I'm getting worse!"

But the truth was, everything that could be done was being done. I'd handled my part. I'd arrived at the hospital quickly. I was in the right place. A false sense of calm had settled over me that Dr. Diaz's ominous second opinion "Don't let anybody touch you" couldn't penetrate. He said that back when my only symptom was tingly lips. And today, according to Dr. Campbell, Dr. Diaz still wasn't willing to operate. The malformation was located deep in "high real estate" -- the brain stem. I didn't research it at the time to avoid scaring myself silly, but I've since learned that the brain stem controls reflex actions and essential internal functions such as breathing and heartbeat. To operate at all was to take incredible risk.

I had something rare. Extremely rare. Technically, I was having a stroke. Not the "ischemic" kind that older people tend to get. Those are caused by a blood clot traveling to the brain. I was having a "hemorrhagic" stroke, in which a bleed in the brain is caused by a malformation or an aneurysm. Arteriovenous malformations, or AVMs, are one type of malformation. Of all strokes, only thirteen percent are hemorrhagic. Of those thirteen percent, only two percent are caused by AVM's. What I had was rarer still. Add to that the location of this malformation, and it's no wonder I had hurried up to wait. Even the brain surgeons were looking for a brain surgeon.

Vivian, Lee Anne and I spent the morning in the little room. We were all cutting up and I was in good spirits. I reported in my slurred way that this was "fucked up." I marveled at everything that happened to me with the curiosity of an outside observer, rather than someone whose life was in danger. The mangled pizza incident had caused me momentary concern. Of far greater concern was that Viv was about to call my parents, specifically my mother.

I'm not the kind of person who falls ill and immediately wants, and can only be comforted by, my mommy. My mother isn't a particularly nurturing person. Well, compared to my father she is. When I was a child, she gave lots of hugs and kisses and said "I love you." She always got after my father to hold, comfort or talk to me. She's wonderful at the showing and the saying. She's rather less inclined to be good at the doing. Home-cooked meals and band-aiding boo-boos were not her things. I grew up to be very independent.

Maybe I strove for the normalcy my father represented. Maybe I tried to maintain some control as things fell apart that day, something I did more easily with my people-pleasing father than my strong-willed mother. Or maybe, as I've told my friends over the years, it was simply that my mother drove me crazy.

Whatever the reason, I begged Viv not to call her. When she insisted, being more aware of my dire condition than I, we compromised. She'd leave my mother a message to update her, she'd tell my father to get here quick.

I don't remember my father's arrival or anything after that. Viv and Lee Anne report that while I was getting a CT scan, they all went to lunch. That seems so *regular*. But just because I was in the middle of my own personal disaster, doesn't mean the world stopped spinning. People still had to eat, right? I wouldn't eat again for two months. Or see the outside world, except from a hospital window or parking lot, for five months. I don't recall what that final meal had been. It could've been Chef Boyardee out of a can for all I know. That would seem like fine dining in the months to come.

By the time the three returned, I'd lost the ability to speak. The blood in my brain had wiped out another critical function and I was drowning in silence. Lee Anne says I was still quite expressive with my eyes and I got mad that everyone was talking about me, but not to me. She came over to repeat what the doctors said. I was to be life-flighted to Gainesville. They'd found someone to do the surgery the next day. Viv called her husband to say if he wanted to see me alive, he should come now.

She also called my emergency contacts and then some. She called my mother back. My mom, dad and Danielle would fly from South Florida. Rob, Riley, Viv, and Lee Anne would all make the drive from Jacksonville. They were all en route to see if I'd weather through.

Part I: Crisis

HURRICANE WARNING

"Do you want a washcloth over your eyes?" the technician at Beaches MRI asked me.

"No, thank you."

Seconds later, in a space the size of a coffin, I mashed the button in my hand and she slid me back out.

"I looked up," I said. What greeted me was the sight of the top panel of the contraption I'd been lying in, only inches away from my nose. Once my eyes had opened, there was no more lying to my brain. I was suffocating, trapped.

The technician smiled. "That's what the washcloth's for."

It was late August and my first MRI. They had asked me if I was claustrophobic. I'd said no. It was getting harder to breathe. "Do you think I'm claustrophobic?"

"Lord, no," the round black woman with warm eyes said. "If you were, you'd know it. I've seen 'em 'bout to come off this table."

I thought about it. I felt pretty ready to leap. The panic button grew moist in my hand. Or the call button. That's what they called it. I added the panic.

She slid me back in with the washcloth in place and instructions to count to 500, not to move and not to look up. This time, I listened.

After various counts, she let me out to make sure I wasn't going crazy and once to inject dye into my arm. After 45 minutes, I was done. I survived.

I wonder what kind of treatment I would have received if I *was* claustrophobic. Can they knock you out? If so, I think it's worth the lie. Years later, I read about a man stuck in an MRI machine when the power went out. He had to wait in there until the power came back on. My organs seize just thinking about it.

The technician lady gave me a big hug goodbye. I should have known right then it was bad news. Those technicians see everything on the film. They know.

Back at my apartment, my two cats, Ben and Bella, greeted me at the door. The apartment was a nice perk of my job. I worked as a massage therapist and gave three hours of chair massage a week to fellow residents of the apartment complex in exchange for a whopping $500 off rent. I had moved in earlier that summer. It was the kind of deal I couldn't refuse since I could no longer afford the mortgage payments on my house near the beach.

It had been a sad year, beginning with the passing of my cat, Merrill, in October of 2005. Merrill was my one and only, my steady companion since I moved to Jacksonville out of college in 1992. He was 13 years old.

After Merrill died, I ended a three year relationship with Rob, the man I lived with at the beach. Though I hated to admit it, my mother was right. I couldn't afford the house on a massage therapist's salary without Rob's contribution. When I'd bought it, I was in love, working at a high paying marketing job and operating under the assumption that things would simply work out like they always did. So, I ignored my mother's financial advice and changed careers. By the spring of 2006, I'd run up my credit cards and refinanced the house twice. Things weren't exactly working out.

Research reveals life's greatest stressors: death, divorce and moving. Within a year, I experienced all three. Merrill wasn't just a cat, he was my child, the only child I ever wanted. And Rob and I weren't married, but we shared a life together. And then there was the move.

I organized a garage sale to slim down my possessions from what filled a three-bedroom house to what would furnish a two-bedroom apartment. I felt embarrassed by my welling tears when a man asked the price of the print Rob and I had hung over our bed. In it, a couple stood on a Mediterranean balcony overlooking the water at sunset. The figures, drawn in skinny silhouette, even looked like us, their heads jutting forward over long necks. And in the corner of the frame, a cat. *Pareja y Gato*. Couple and Cat. That had been us. Now it was just me.

The people renting the house asked if they could move some items into the garage ahead of time. I felt nauseated watching them and retreated to the side shed to lock up some things. The next door neighbor peered over the fence at me. Though we hadn't become good friends, we were friendly enough. Her husband had run credit checks on the new tenants for me.

"Are you doing okay?" she asked. A stay-at-home mom, baby burps and after school snacks stained her frumpy top.

"Did you see the size of that TV?" I responded. It was beastly. It must have been ninety-inches wide. It took four men to roll the monstrosity into the house. She nodded as I continued. "Boys. Why did I rent to boys? And with a dog! What was I thinking?"

I hadn't been thinking. Not about the house anyway, just about saving money. That sweet little beach house with its fireplace and hardwood floors and little herb garden by the kitchen door. Merrill liked to sit outside under the jasmine that dripped off the fence while I planted rows of thyme and basil. There was even a patch of catnip.

After downsizing I settled for potted plants and hung my wind chimes on a six by ten balcony that never got enough breeze to move them. And I scolded Ben, the kitten, when he ran up the screen. I sighed and sat on the Adirondack chair that used to look out over a garden and bird bath. The bird bath was one of the things I'd locked away, along with my gardening tools, in the shed at the side of the house.

In truth, I was mildly depressed. Not can't-get-out-of-bed depressed, just a steady constantly-on-the-verge-of-tears depressed. Always sad. Come to think of it, I didn't really want to get out of bed, either. I dreaded seeing my clients and no matter what time I finally got going, I always wished I'd scheduled them later. I wanted to spend my mornings taking nice long walks on the beach and eating Cocoa Puffs in front of *The Price Is Right*.

In hindsight, I was on top of the world. With no way of knowing what was to come, I focused on my current problems. I was 36 and could rack up yet another failed relationship. I struggled financially and felt burned out in a career I'd just begun. I moved away from the beachside community I loved and lost my cat of 13 years.

And then there was the tingling numbness that had started in my lips in July and spread to my right cheek by late August. The neurologist ordered the MRI "just to start ruling things out." That same neurologist called me on Monday morning of the following week -- "I didn't call on Friday because I wanted you to have a worry-free weekend." I try to recall that last, supposedly blissful, weekend often. I have no idea what I did. Probably laid on the couch, feeling sad and eating chocolate frosting out of the can with a spoon. It's impossible, really, to be truly grateful for what you have, while you have it.

And so, wallowing in self-pity, I was still in bed when she called well after nine.

While I may have been depressed on the surface, deep down I was optimistic. I did not view the news as the worst. The worst would be cancer. But the malformation growing in my brain stem and pressing on a facial nerve was not a tumor. It was a mass of blood vessels that had probably been around since my birth "and had bled out into the brain about every ten years," speculated the first neurosurgeon.

Looking back, I think it's fair to say, Dr. Anthony Campbell was quite egotistical. He said he did almost this exact type of surgery all the time and estimated my recovery time to be "about six weeks." In his opinion, and I agreed, better to do brain surgery now and remove the malformation, than to wait for the next bleed to cause "unknown neurological deficits," which I correctly assumed to be scary stuff. As in not being able to write or walk.

Of course, the next bleed might never come. But, there was evidence it had bled before, maybe three times in my life, the most recent time causing my lips and right side of my face to go numb. I had never known about it before because it hadn't caused any symptoms or done any damage until the numbness. But, it was growing. Each time a bleed occurred, the blood, being small in amount, dissipated and was absorbed back into my body, leaving a cavity or depression that filled with spinal fluid. This allowed the "cavernous angioma" to grow.

This is exactly how I explained it to my mom on the phone, the evening after the first opinion. She freaked out. Granted, I'd had more time to adjust. I sat on my friend Vivian's back porch, drinking a glass of wine. My mom hadn't had a drink in 13 years and I hoped I wasn't giving her reason to start. I handed Vivian the phone, my patience already spent. Viv was a nurse and had accompanied me to the appointment with Dr. Campbell to help me decipher the medical jargon and remember what he said. She relished the role and was good at it. Let her deal with my mother.

Viv and I had it all figured out. Talking it over with family and getting a second opinion were just technicalities. Telling my mom and other family members was just part of the process. I would go down to Miami, where my mom lived, for the second opinion of a Dr. Jorge Diaz, as advised by Dr. Campbell. Mom would go with me to that appointment so she could ask all the questions she wanted. Then, I'd come back to Jacksonville for surgery with Dr. Campbell - and do my six week recovery time at Vivian and her husband Carl's house.

Vivian and I thought this was best. Viv invited me to stay in their guest room, where I'd already spent many a late night. Bella and Ben had even been invited, bringing the grand animal total of the Conner residence to one dog and five cats. We had it all planned.

Good friends said I was handling it well --- impending brain surgery. As crazy as it sounds, I looked forward to the break. A break from working, a break from clients, a break from trying (and failing) to make enough money. A break from routine. It was like growing up in Miami when school let out early for a hurricane. It was exciting. We were just happy to be out of school early. We weren't worried about the approaching storm. We didn't really think our lives would be turned upside down or changed forever. It would probably turn at the last minute.

LABEL ME ANNOYED

My mom quit drinking in 1992. Hurricane Andrew hit Miami in August of that year and she moved from the suburbs of Kendall to South Beach. It was the only place she could find an apartment while our townhouse was rebuilt. By the time it was finished she was there to stay. She'd found her new favorite neighborhood. She also found out she was an alcoholic and a lesbian. Well, I found out. I'm sure a part of her had always known. It was actual news to me.

At first I thought it was just one more thing she had latched on to, like the various get-rich-quick schemes throughout my child-hood. She was a little flaky and South Beach was more than a little trendy. Everyone in South Beach was gay and recovering from some-thing. Maybe she was just trying to fit in.

But when I really thought about it, the signs had been there. I re-examined old scenes that had seemed trivial to my childish mind. Now the memories were infused with new meaning as the picture became whole. Like the dinners that burned on the stove because she "fell asleep." Or the neighborly camaraderie that mysteriously dis-solved into dirty looks and drive-bys when my mom started hanging out with one of the two women who lived together down the street.

You'd think these things were obvious, but you'd be wrong. My mother was a functioning alcoholic and a happy drunk. There were no screaming rampages nor throwing of dishes. Sure, she called in late a lot, but she managed to keep her job. She was a middle management supervisor of county employees and there were far worse fuck-ups in the county.

And there were plenty of reasons for my parents' marriage to fall apart. I wouldn't even call her preference for women one of the main ones, though it may well have been. I'm sure my father would call it The Reason, since doing so alleviates any need for accountability on his part.

So it came as a bit of a surprise when my mother, at the age of 52, embraced both these things about herself. I did what any good, liberal-minded daughter would do.

"Congratulations, Mom. If you're happy, I'm happy."

Curious friends asked me if she had a girlfriend. Not that I knew of. Hey, I'm accepting, let's not push it. She *is* my mother. That would be too weird. Besides, I was a selfish twenty-something, engrossed in my own life and she had self-admitted intimacy issues. We left it at that.

From where I stood, the lesbianism wasn't the problem -- the alcoholism was. Or more accurately, the sobriety. It drove a wedge between us much further than the 350 miles that separated us. And so began my love/hate relationship with Alcoholics Anonymous.

Most importantly, it worked. There was no falling off the wagon. My mother jumped on board and never looked back. But I wondered privately if she wasn't just trading one dependency for another. Albeit, a healthier one. She went to a meeting every day in the beginning. Sometimes two or three. And when she wasn't attending a meeting with her fellow recovering alcoholics, she grabbed coffee or a movie with them. After she had been there for a while, she acted as a mentor to other recovering alcoholics. At one point, she was a sponsor to twelve newcomers. *Twelve.* I heard her speaking to them on the phone in hushed tones during my visits. She dedicated herself to recovery.

Her speech became peppered with various euphemisms picked up at AA. "God willing" particularly irritated me. I told her on the phone what day I planned to arrive for a visit. "God willing," she interjected. I was going to a concert with my boyfriend. "God willing," came the response.

Terms like "enabler" and "co-dependent" were now part of her everyday vocabulary. I became fluent in recovery-speak. You couldn't help someone become sober. They had to want it for themselves. Usually, they had to hit rock bottom first. I also was well-versed in the steps. Step 1: We admitted we were powerless over alcohol -- that our lives had become unmanageable. It wasn't enough not to drink. It was far better to "have a program." You had to work the steps. Those who didn't were "dry drunks." My mother knew lots of dry drunks.

In recovery, my mother became infinitely wiser. Or so she thought. It was during this time that she began to drive me crazy. While advice to take "one day at a time" might be sound and her statement that "there are no coincidences" might be true, these catchphrases weren't a real help. Sometimes I really just wanted to gossip. My mother didn't gossip anymore.

I was made aware that as her daughter, I had a label of my own. I was an Adult Child of an Alcoholic, and as such, there was virtually no end to the ways in which I might be screwed up. My mother was ever vigilant in looking for signs that this was the case. In a Barnes and Noble, she picked up a copy of the self-help book that would define me. I read the back cover. Adult children of alcoholics lie when it would be just as easy to tell the truth. *Not me.* Adult children of alcoholics have difficulty having fun. *I don't.* Adult children of alcoholics are super responsible or super irresponsible. *Okay, maybe I am responsible, but super responsible?* I almost missed a plane for a new job training because I'd been out partying the night before and showed up to meet the CEO with the worst hangover of my life. How responsible was that? Okay, maybe an alcohol-related incident isn't the best example here.

I handed the book back to her. "Mom, I'm fine."

"You know what fine means, don't you?"

I was about to be treated to another pearl of AA wisdom. "What?"

"Fucked up, Insecure, Neurotic and Emotional," she recited.

I managed a weak smile. In the end, she decided I was in denial.

The worst part was that I lacked someone to talk to about it. My mom had been one of my main confidants. She suggested Al-Anon and I'm sure would have been thrilled to have another 12-stepper in the family, but I didn't feel it was the place for me. I thought Al-Anon was more for people who *lived* with an alcoholic. Maybe, if she'd gotten sober when I was still in high school. As it was, I saw my mom three times a year. I couldn't have much in common with the spouses or younger children of these people, could I? I wasn't directly affected by it anymore. Besides, my biggest problem wasn't the drinking, it was the recovery. It hardly seemed that the place to complain about a 12-step program was another 12-step program.

It was hard to talk to any of my friends about it. My mom was the cool mom that my friends talked to instead of their own parents. Everyone loved my mom. "I'd kill to have your mom. Wanna trade?" I heard whenever I grumbled. It was hard to explain what bothered me about it so much. And then it happened. The thing that put my mom's stability in question, even in the eyes of my friends. She renamed the dog.

Our dog was an Australian Shepherd that we got sometime during my high school years. We named him Rhett, after the hero in *Gone With The Wind,* the movie I loved and we watched together every year.

One visit, I returned home and my mother introduced me to our beloved dog -- William, renamed in at least his seventh year, after Bill Wilson, the founder of AA. I had gone along with many a thing lately. This would not be one of them.

"Mom, you changed his name?"

"He really didn't seem like a Rhett, you know?"

No, I did not know. Nor did I want it explained to me.

"Look," she said, brightening. "He knows it. Here, William. C'mere boy!" The dog came to her, wagging his tail.

I got down on the floor. "C'mere Rhett. Here, Rhett!" He turned and came to me.

I'm sure she called him William most of the time. But during those few visits a year, he was Rhett/William.

The name changing was a detail that I doled out to a select few and only when I really needed someone to see what I was dealing with. It worked surprisingly well. I found myself feeling defensive on my mother's behalf.

Only I'm allowed to call my mother crazy -- no one else is.

I spilled out the truth in my journal at night. It was my confessional. Hi. My name is Amy and my mother's sobriety is making me insane. Hi, Amy! Maybe the first step was admitting I had a problem.

THE CALM BEFORE

"Turn right *there*," I said, as my mother sped by the street.

"Crap, Amy. Give me a little notice." She swerved into a driveway marked for emergency vehicles only.

"I didn't know it was coming up so fast. It's not like I've been there before," I said.

"Well, you're the one with the directions."

"If you slowed down, you'd have time to turn." Then, throwing my hands up, "This is the emergency room entrance."

"I know that. Don't you think I know that?" She shifted her black Volkswagen bug into reverse, then drove back onto the main road and through the intersection just as the light turned red.

"Nice," I said.

"What? That was yellow." A car behind us honked.

"Whatever you say." It's what I said whenever I was giving up the argument. To show I was the bigger person. That she was impossible to reason with. She hated this.

We were both a bit cranky in the heat. It was the beginning of fall, but in Miami, it was still scorching. I'd been home for three days and was usually scouting out high bridges by day two. Add to that the reason for my visit and it's no surprise we couldn't find the place, even with my neat Mapquest printout and carefully highlighted route.

We were lost on the grounds of Miami Jackson Memorial Hospital for the second opinion of Dr. Jorge Diaz -- brain surgeon extraordinaire. I'd gotten his name from Dr. Campbell, who'd been his student. My mom also had a friend who worked as a nurse at Jackson. The friend agreed. He was the best.

This seemed to be confirmed by the number of people in the waiting room, once we found it. It felt like being in another country. Spanish and English mixed in the air. People came from everywhere to get the opinion of this man. Not just Miami or Florida. Not even just the United States. The woman seated on the other side of my mother flew from Brazil.

In the time it took to arrange my purse and MRI film next to me on the floor, my mother had gotten this woman's complete medical history. And given her mine. My mother filled me in as the woman looked on. "Helene's been told she has an inoperable brain tumor, but she came to get Dr. Diaz's opinion," she said.

"Oh," I said.

Good grief. What was I supposed to say to that?

She'd done it again. Gotten someone else's life story in under a minute. My mother didn't just buy milk at the Quick Mart, she also extracted that the cashier had just moved into town to get away from the abusive ex who she met through her cousin and was now locked in a bitter custody battle with. Over their three-year-old daughter. Named Marie. After the cashier's grandmother.

Maybe the poor woman didn't feel like sharing her inoperable brain tumor with complete strangers. Just like I didn't feel like sharing what my mother was now telling her.

"Amy has a malformation in her brain stem," she said. They went on chatting about my brain.

Truth is, the only one usually put off by all this candid talk was me. People don't seem to mind opening up to her. They seem to welcome it.

When we finally saw Dr. Diaz, I was struck by two things. First, how different he was from Dr. Campbell. Dr. Campbell had mentioned he'd studied under Dr. Diaz, but even if I hadn't known this, there was no mistaking who was the teacher and who was the student. Everything about Dr. Diaz screamed brain surgeon. From his expensive-looking suit to the way he carried himself, he just naturally commanded respect. I'd been tempted to flirt with the handsome Dr. Campbell in his white coat. I wouldn't dream of doing the same with Dr. Diaz. Even the "hi" that Dr. Campbell had asked me to pass on, now seemed juvenile and pathetic. There was no question what this doctor's time was worth and I fought the urge to scramble away as if we'd already taken up too much of it. Second, I was struck by his last words to me as we left the office. "Don't let anybody touch you."

Don't let anybody touch me? This was bad news. Not because it gave me a better grasp of the gravity of my situation. The facts were registering, but only as they applied to someone else's brain, someone else's life. I didn't seem to absorb information as it pertained to my physical well-being at all. No, this was bad news because now there was no clear plan of action. The strategy Viv and I had worked out on her back porch had started to unravel. I would need a third opinion.

Mom and I sat on the bench outside the office before beginning the trek to the car. We'd come in the wrong entrance and now had a long walk back, if we could find where we'd parked.

"So, that's that," my mother said.

"What's that?"

"You heard the man. Don't let anybody touch you means don't let anybody touch you."

"Mom ---"

"Amy, this is one of the best brain surgeons in the country."

I took a deep breath. She was scared. "With *one* opinion," I said. "So far, we have two completely opposite opinions. Yes, Dr. Diaz's weighs more, but we need a third."

She knew I was right. We were both rational people. Her mother bear claws had come out in an instant, but she pulled them back in. "Okay."

It was the logical thing to do, yes. But deep down, I wanted someone to agree with the cocky Dr. Campbell. I wanted the surgery. I considered myself an optimist, not a pessimist. I didn't want to spend my future waiting for something bad to happen, worrying every time I hit my head or got a headache. Becoming a hypochondriac. That was no way to live.

I would get my wish, though not at all in the way I expected. I drove back to Jacksonville the next day. I planned on spending the next month setting up an appointment and getting that third opinion. As it turned out, I didn't have that long.

A PEACOCK CHRISTMAS

The Christmas tree is artificial. Obviously. It's sparkly silver. That doesn't mean it has a perfect shape, though. It looks like it might have been purchased at a yard sale. It's missing several branches and there are two gaping holes that I can see from my vantage point at the side of the room. A man in a tight T-shirt sits to a smattering of applause as I continue looking at the tree. It's draped with garland that looks suspiciously like purple boas, and there are peacock feathers dripping from most every branch. Those that don't have shimmering feathers have shiny purple or gold balls. I am blinded and mesmerized at once. It's like staring at a solar eclipse.

Christmas morning, 1999. I drove home for the holiday. I'm counting the days until I drive back to Jacksonville. It's not that I don't like spending time with my mom. I do. But we don't really do that anymore. Not just the two of us. Now, we spend time with all her new friends. Which is why I find myself at the South Beach Gay and Lesbian meeting of Alcoholics Anonymous on an uncomfortable metal folding chair instead of on the floor under a normal-looking tree eating candy canes in my pajamas.

If I sound bitter - I am. It's *Christmas* morning. I didn't drive five-and-a-half hours to be company to a bunch of strangers' misery.

I came to eat cookies for breakfast, see *It's A Wonderful Life* and watch the cats get high on their new catnip toys.

My mother walks to the podium and I pay attention. She's telling the slip story. I'm glad she chose to lighten the mood. It is a funny story. I've heard it before, but my mother tells it so well. Basically, it goes that she was so hungover, probably still drunk in fact, that she rode the Metrorail all the way to work one morning and sat down in her cubicle only to realize she was wearing her black slip as a skirt. She had to ride all the way home to change. Humiliation is a story they all seem to share.

She takes her seat to an explosion of applause mixed with appreciative chuckles. The meeting adjourns by gathering in a circle, and I am holding hands with two people I've never met. I mumble my way through the prayer about the daily bread, and we come to a chant I can say confidently, if not as enthusiastically as everyone else.

"It works if you work it! So work it, it's worth it!" My clasped hands are being pumped every few syllables.

"Let's eat!" someone says.

There are two things I love about hanging out with lots of gay men. First, everyone's a gourmet chef. The group converges on two long folding tables that someone has covered with red and green plaid paper tablecloths.

There is carved turkey and a roasted duck. There are wild mushrooms with crab inside and stuffing with cranberries. There is every kind of salad. Shrimp salad. Artichoke salad. Mozzarella and tomato salad. And salad salad, which doesn't appear to be going too fast.

I grab a plate and start filling it. I hit the desserts first. They're all homemade. Christmas cookies, macadamia nut cookies, peanut butter fudge. There are fluffy lemon bars with marshmallows. And the star of the show -- an entire gingerbread house. It even has window boxes with gumdrop flowers. It's an edible fairytale. Someone had a lot of time on their hands.

"*Suz-anne!*" I hear someone call my mother's name in a sing-song voice. She has fallen into line behind me. "You didn't tell us your daughter was so *gor-geous!*"

This is the other thing I love about gay men. The compliments. I've heard "cute" or "pretty" before, but those are average words around here. These guys aren't into accuracy so much as the triple word score. They throw around superlatives like beads off a gay pride float at Mardi Gras. Everything is *fab-u-lous.* Everything has an exclamation point.

My mother introduces me to Joe, the interior designer, and man responsible for the peacock feathers.

"We just *l-ove* your mother," he tells me. There appears to be only one other lesbian in the group and she has the personality of white walls. Of course they love my mother.

We exchange pleasantries and it's back to the food. I add shrimp salad and some greens to my plate. It would be healthy if it weren't for the mound of desserts.

I am just about to bite the head off a snowman when a man approaches me and my mom. He is wearing short shorts, a Santa hat and eyeliner.

"Your mother is the most wonderful person in the world," he says.

My mother introduces me to her "dear friend Tom" and turns to embrace him. They stand locked in a long hug, slowly rocking back and forth.

My mom's a big hugger now. She was always affectionate with family, but this penchant for hugging everyone is something I think she picked up from AA, or "in the rooms" as they say. I am wondering whether or not it would be rude to take a bite of my cookie when they finally break apart.

"Your mother was really there for me and I'll never forget it," Tom says. His eyes are glistening, threatening to ruin his makeup. They are standing with their arms wrapped around each other.

Who is this guy again?

"Tom was the first person I met here at the clubhouse," my mom says.

"Back when we were both fucked up, if you'll pardon my French," Tom says. "Well, *more* fucked up."

They burst out laughing. I smile.

"Always working on ourselves!" he says with a roll of his eyes.

"It's not exactly the Mental Health Olympics around here, is it?" my mom laughs.

No, it's not, I think.

Something similar to that exchange is echoed around the clubhouse until I have met almost everyone. Although, I couldn't pick any of them out from any of the other men strolling the sidewalks or eating at the cafes of South Beach's Lincoln Road. Everyone is a dear friend. Everyone thinks my mother is so special. I must be the luckiest girl in the world to have such a mother.

I don't feel very lucky. I feel like a jealous schoolgirl.

I'm the only family member, the only outsider. I think about her bringing me here. At first, it seems like bad judgment on her part. Then I realize maybe all of these men have nowhere else to go, are estranged from family members. Maybe they would never invite family into their sanctuary.

I *am* lucky. We are unique in that my mother can share this with me.

I am enjoying a brief moment of solitude, finishing a few bites of salad and reading the walls. There's a sign-up list with lots of chores, in case you thought staying sober was the only duty here. Someone is responsible for coffee, folks are needed for clean-up, and a person has to welcome newcomers at the door. Once inside, you are greeted by several signs with slogans. There are the usual of course, "One Day at a Time" and "Easy Does It," but there is also the unexpected and profound, "Time Takes Time." I'm still trying to wrap my brain around this one when my mom announces it's time to go.

I hope we are going home. I want nothing more than to kick off my shoes and collapse on the couch. But I'm disappointed.

We spend the rest of the day flitting from non-alcoholic party to non-alcoholic party. These people never stop. They're always busy. Last night, we attended The Gay Men's Chorus. I had hoped for say, a tongue in cheek production of *Guys and Dolls: Guys and Guys*, but it turned out the chorus took itself way too seriously for that. We were treated to an evening of no-nonsense seasonal music.

By the time we enter the third party, I'm praying for somebody's wayward, drunk cousin to show me the secret batch of spiked eggnog in the back room. And I don't even like eggnog.

Why must we keep up this pace? Doesn't anyone ever enjoy a little downtime?

Gay men are always on. Way on. Laughing, teasing, singing, joking. Then I notice I'm the only one who isn't an alcoholic and begin to put it together. It's just like the remedy for a broken heart - keep busy. Only here, everyone is trying to outrun their pain and not drink. They've got to be twice as fast.

It's dusk before we're finally on our way home and I'm thinking about how different my Christmas turned out to be from

Thanksgiving at my father's house. Christmas trees at my dad's in Hobe Sound, Florida, have never been dressed in purple boas like their South Beach counterparts. And while visiting my father, I may meet "Mom," the eighty-seven-year-old waitress at Mom's Diner, but never Ernesto the cross-dressing drag queen.

My mom opens the door to her condo and turns on some lights. She flicks on the television and kneels down to switch on the Christmas tree lights. A marathon of *A Christmas Story* is playing and Ralphie is just about to get his wish. I flop on the couch. It's a move I've anticipated all day. My mom settles down beside me and brings a plastic tray of Publix Christmas cookies. She breaks into the cellophane and tells me again how when she was little she wanted a Daisy Red Ryder Rifle too, and bought herself one in her early fifties. She picks out a few cookies, careful to leave my favorites, the sprinkled red bells and green trees. I gaze at the tree and notice a few shiny peacock feathers peering back at me under the twinkling lights.

"You got feathers too?" I ask.

"Leftovers. They only came in bags of a hundred." This confirms my suspicion. They looked too uniform to be real, but I wouldn't put it past those guys to have a couple of actual peacocks strutting around the clubhouse yard.

One of my mom's cats is batting around a piece of wrapping paper from early this morning. We laugh at his antics as the balled up paper skitters across the floor. I settle farther into the couch and crunch on a cookie.

"Merry Christmas, Amy Q. I'm glad you're here," my mom says.

So am I.

BFF

I was a terrible maid of honor. I kept forgetting to fix her train and hold her flowers. She dragged me away from the reception. Being properly (or improperly) drunk by then had rendered me useless at helping her pack for the honeymoon. Danielle had followed some antiquated "101 Things To Do for a Perfect Wedding." It called for my helping her pack and change into her "bridal traveling suit" before she and Frank waved goodbye and rode off in a tin-can-trailing limousine. Instead, we went back to her apartment where she stuffed things into a bag as I rifled through the contents of her fridge and complained about missing my piece of wedding cake. Apparently, driving through Krystal's was too much to ask a bride on her wedding day. I munched on some Oreos. There was also the great speech debacle, the embarrassment of which didn't cause me too much concern that night but still makes me cringe decades later.

Danielle had assured me I wouldn't have to give a toast at the wedding reception. So I mustered up the courage to give a short version to the small crowd at the rehearsal dinner. The story of how she and Frank met made the perfect toast. It guaranteed laughter in all the right places.

Danielle and I were in the tenth grade when a friend set me up with Frank. I was supposed to meet him at the Haagen-Dazs in the mall where he worked when, as I told it, I "made the mistake" of bringing Danielle. They met, fell in love, and now we were gathered here today. Frank and I probably wouldn't have had a first date, let alone a second. I wasn't his type and he wasn't mine. Still, it made a cute story. *At the rehearsal dinner.*

Unfortunately, no one told the best man or the deejay that I was off the hook for telling it at the reception. In a moment that stands out in my memory as the longest moment in time, the best man extended me the microphone and a spotlight shone down in a room of over 200 people. I think I was introduced, but it's hard to say because my ears had stopped working properly, and what sound there was in the quiet room came from very far away. I did the only thing a shocked and petrified girl of 23 could do. Nothing. I shook my head and refused to take the mic. It seemed an eternity before this was understood and I was released from the spotlight. Another awkward minute or two later, the music started up.

The other bridesmaids could've told Danielle something like this was bound to happen. I was unfit. This much was clear when I refused to have my stubby nails adorned with acrylic tips and painted with Aphrodite's Rose like all the other bridesmaids. The Boca girls did all the work -- helped Danielle pick the dress, flowers and invitations -- then I swept in from out of town to take the glory. This was how I figured they saw it.

Danielle was resolute. I was her maid of honor. We decided this at 13, living in neighboring housing complexes in the suburbs of southwest Miami. We'd grown into different people, but our friendship was born of a shared history. We'd been best friends since a time when all that friendship required was proximity, a shared love of the material girl, and exasperation with our mothers, who we were certain were trying to ruin our lives.

Complaining about our mothers was how we spent a lot of our time. We swapped horror stories at the large wall that divided Pine Tree Village (where Mom and I moved after the divorce) from Sable Chase (where Danielle lived). I would climb up the wall by way of the A/C unit and wait for her to come running across the road. Though we each grumbled about our own mothers, we sought refuge with the others.

Danielle's mom was a "50s mom," while mine was more from the 60s.

I headed to Danielle's house for balanced meals and help with my homework. She came to mine for junk food and straight answers. (Had my mom ever smoked pot?) Dinners at Danielle's were always sit down affairs with a protein, a starch and a vegetable. There were warm rolls in a basket on the table followed by algebra lessons with her dad (or chemistry as we moved into high school). At my house, Danielle and I ordered pizza and baked cookies from a chilled log. We rented R-rated movies that we weren't allowed to watch at Danielle's or just talked. We could tell my mom anything and my friends told me how lucky I was to have such a "cool" mom. A fact I didn't appreciate till much later.

I still have a picture, snapped by my mom, of Danielle and me at 15, in front of that wall. Unofficial cheerleaders, we waved homemade signs and teal-colored pompoms at passing vehicles to support the Miami Dolphins and Dan Marino on their way to the Super Bowl. We squealed when a car honked. Looking at that picture, I'm struck by our youth and how impossibly skinny our limbs were. Two gangly colts, who had yet to grow into any beauty.

But that would come. Particularly for Danielle. By college, with her long, blonde hair and cool, turquoise eyes, she was the closest approximation to a real, live Barbie doll I've ever seen. We were in a restaurant years ago, when she actually *was* mistaken for Barbie. A little girl, who looked five or six, shyly approached our table with an apologetic-looking mother behind her mouthing the word "sorry."

"Barbie?" she asked. Sure. Barbie and her brunette friend sharing a massive plate of cheese fries at Applebee's. We drove over in the pink convertible.

With her mother's prodding, the little girl asked for an autograph, which Danielle granted with a gracious smile, signing 'Barbie' on a napkin in loopy cursive with a heart dotting the 'i.' I stared open-mouthed at Danielle over the whole scene, but she shrugged it off. This wasn't even the first time it had happened.

"You should've worked at Disney," I said, returning to the fries. "You could've been Cinderella."

Though they clearly were a matched set, Frank was no Ken doll. Especially not the effeminate version that would come later in *Toy Story 3*. Typically tall, dark and handsome, he and Danielle would make beautiful children together. I was touched that their three boys were growing up with the knowledge that I was a special family friend, due in no small part to Danielle always handing them the phone, coaching them to say they loved and missed me.

Her son Max had just returned the phone to Danielle when I told her what Dr. Diaz had said. It had been about a week since I'd been to Miami for the second opinion. "Don't let anybody touch you?!" she shouted into the receiver. "What the hell's that supposed to mean?" Danielle had a tendency toward excitement.

"It means, I have to get a third opinion."

With each other, we reverted back to 13 year-olds. Conversations with Danielle were always loud and a little shrill.

When I briefly dated her brother-in-law, we fantasized about the wedding that would make us real sisters. There was no one else on earth I could be so, well … *girly* with. Actually, 'dated' is a bit of an overstatement about the brother-in-law. He's an actor in L.A. How close could we be?

She brings out a different side of me. An important side. In the years to come, I would increasingly value the loyalty she brought to our friendship. Just like she did at her wedding. If I had it to do over again, I'd paint my nails in Aphrodite's Rose and take the microphone.

MORPHINE DREAMS

Once it became clear I'd survived surgery, I was transported to a room in the Intensive Care Unit of Shands Hospital, Gainesville. There, I became known as the girl who gave the finger. Apparently, I flipped off a bunch of doctors and nurses, probably some student interns too. I'm not sure why, but they must have deserved it.

Staff drugged me with morphine until I learned to express my distaste for it. I shook my head wildly and my eyes bugged out. "No! Not morphine!" I managed to mouth. The hellish nightmares, worse with the painkiller, usually involved hoards of people draped around my hospital room -- behind the door, on the ceiling, in the bed. Scary, sloth-like strangers. Everywhere. Watching.

Not that I had any room to talk. I was pretty scary and sloth-like myself. Only half of my head was shaved. A fresh incision was closed with little black staples that my hairdresser found and pulled out even seven months later. The other half was in the chin-length bob I'd worn into the ER. It hung in greasy strings, unwashed for weeks and sticky with my own drool.

When The Mortal God Who Had Saved My Life showed up with his fledglings taking their copious notes, my mother reminded Dr. Lewis about my hair. There was a rule about no sharp objects next to my head (imagine that). No one except Dr. Lewis could place the order to shave the half bob and even things out. Somehow, permission was never granted. Brain surgeons have any number of life and death matters to tend to that outrank the problem of my hairstyle, so I remained, day after day, part cancer patient, part drugged-out hippie, until my mother took charge of the situation.

Riley offered to sneak in his electric razor, and my mom agreed to the plan. In a covert operation in which my mother guarded the door, Riley buzzed the right side of my head to match the left.

Greg Riley was a friend of Rob's. I called him Riley because that's what Rob called him, in that cool guy way males refer to other males. Riley driving to Gainesville during my time there was both an accident and a miracle. While I made the transition from walking and talking person to bed-ridden mute in the Jacksonville ER, Viv had called him from my phone just to get Rob's number. Such is your fate when you're the ex-boyfriend -- no one knows how to reach you. I'd taken Rob off my speed dial, calling his number by heart instead.

Riley was the kind of guy that should've had a girlfriend but never did. In some ways, I found him more desirable than Rob. With dark hair and a light scattering of tattoos, he looked like a bad boy without actually being one. I felt the pull one day at the beach as Riley showed me how to kayak in the ocean and I compared his tanned, outdoorsy skin to Rob's pale, computer-guy complexion. But Riley had this way of coming on too strong that always landed him in the friend zone with women. He seemed almost desperate, to want it too bad, and I dreaded going out in a group, where he'd hit on all my friends and they'd complain about it later.

So in the ICU, Riley, the friend of the ex-boyfriend, showed up too. And it was fortunate he did. Riley was a massage therapist who worked for Sunns Rehabilitation alongside physical therapists. He told my mom to apply for the grant that got me into Sunns Rehab Hospital in Jacksonville. We could never have afforded it otherwise, even with health insurance. He had a caring bedside manner and was an invaluable help to my family, but I couldn't help wonder if he saw this as his "in" now that Rob was out of the picture. I don't think I was wrong to assume he liked me. Friends joked that Riley liked everybody. And, like everyone close to me, he saw my situation as a temporary setback. I was now tolerating sitting up in a wheelchair for longer periods of time. I still wasn't transferring, dressing or moving the wheelchair myself, but that's what Sunns was for. I would learn how to walk again. It would be a very long road, but I was determined to travel back and recover the girl I used to be. I think he kept the image of that girl in his head. I know I did.

That's why, in the first week in ICU, news that I was flipping people off was met with happy relief. Everyone delighted, with the possible exception of whoever was being flipped off. It was surely a sign, one of the first, that I was still myself, that I was in there somewhere, underneath all the tubes and beeping machinery.

Though there's some confusion as to who I gave the finger, there is little doubt as to why. I had developed a pet peeve of being talked about like I wasn't there, as if I were a mere lump occupying the bed, incapable of understanding. But I understood. Every word. I just couldn't speak. Which is why I resorted to ... umm ... a more primitive form of communication.

My father reports that when he and my stepmother checked in at the nurses' station, they were asked to wait for the head nurse to tell them what had happened the day before.

"Ohhh, you're her father?" the nurse broke away from a group of employees and came over.

"Yes. Is everything okay?"

"Oh yes. It just seems that she ... responded ... well, it's just that ..."

"Yes?"

"Well, a group of hospital staff was standing in her room talking about their upcoming Halloween party and who was going and what they were all dressing up as ..."

"Yes?"

"Well, one of them turned around and your daughter was ... giving them ... umm ..."

"Giving them what?"

"The finger," she said, eyes on the floor.

"The finger?"

"Yes," said the nurse. "You know. Shooting the bird."

My mother was quite proud. "Amy obviously didn't appreciate it. They shouldn't have been gossiping next to her bed anyway," she said to my father later.

Lee Anne too had witnessed the same irritation. In the Jacksonville ER, she said I began banging my hands on the bed rails with a "very annoyed look" whenever Dr. Campbell began addressing everyone in the room except me.

Though it's easy to figure out what provoked me, there's some discrepancy over who angered me. My parents believed I was sending my big screw you to the group at large. Yet, I remember a particular male doctor being the recipient. Then again, I also thought Jamie, the man I'd been seeing at the time, was trying to kill me. I made Lee Anne throw out the flowers he sent.

Dreams and reality blended in an ongoing freakish drama. When I could vocalize, I screamed at night, "My legs! My legs!" What I couldn't communicate was that my legs were too long for the bed. In order to keep my feet from hanging over, I would bend slightly to one side at the hips and knees. Because I laid like this for so long, it became excruciatingly painful to move my legs the other way. No one could figure out what I was yelling about. It didn't help that the dream accompanying this pain was that I had been strung up in a tree like a deer, hanging upside down, hunting dogs barking in the distance. Anyone trying to investigate the screaming found me restless and babbling about being eaten by dogs.

A lot of my dreams were set in water. I always waded through it or tried to swim. My father was the hero of most of these dreams, helping me or saving me somehow. I attribute these dreams of water to the loss of sensation on my right side. I waited for it to come back, but it never did. The feeling is heavy, like feeling the pull of gravity or trying to move through water with your clothes on.

Reality was grim, but not as horrific as my imagination. When my eyes were open, I saw double. This was not nearly as upsetting as the nystagmus; my pupils bounced up and down making it difficult for anyone to look at me and almost impossible for me to see.

At first, I had a catheter. I progressed to diapers.

Another intimate joy of hospital life was, what I called, "the mucus wand." I'm sure it has a much more dignified and technical name, but I never learned it. The idea is that when a patient can't swallow, as I couldn't, some poor family member has to take this suction wand, not unlike the ones at the dentist's office, and clean your mouth of fluids. All my friends took their turn with the wand. I don't know how they did it. I'd have been gagging myself had I been together enough to realize I was close to choking on my own phlegm.

Somewhere along the way, doctors performed a tracheotomy. An incision was made at the hollow of my throat to allow for insertion of a tube that enabled me to breathe or be hooked up to a ventilator. A tracheotomy serves the same purpose as "intubation," when a tube is inserted through the mouth. Intubation is not surgically invasive or permanent, but it requires constant sedation since it's so uncomfortable. Patients in the ICU often have tracheotomies, particularly when pneumonia is involved. And I had pneumonia twice before heading to Sunns.

Before I was transferred to Sunns in November, Dr. Lewis and his team stood around my bed and marveled at all I had survived. I still had a feeding tube and tracheotomy, but I was talking.

"You gave everyone a scare for awhile there," one of the younger doctors said.

"I remember you," I said. "You're the one that gave me pneumonia by giving me that hamburger!"

The doctor laughed. Clearly, I had an injured brain. But he also cleared his good name. "No, I didn't! I didn't give you pneumonia."

So, I'd made it all up. I hallucinated a hamburger. Could have been worse. At least I didn't flip him off.

MIND-BENDERS

For the first few weeks at Sunns, I thought I was dead. It didn't help matters that three nurses I saw regularly were named Angel, Grace and Faith. Only Hope was missing. Often literally.

I didn't think I was dead all the time. Most of the time, I was perfectly lucid. Or I knew enough to act that way. Then I would take a friend aside and whisper, "You'd tell me if I was dead, right?"

Lee Anne's answer satisfied me. "Girl, if you're dead, then so am I, and I'm pretty sure I'm alive." We laughed and for the time being, I felt content.

Rob, however, was the wrong person to consult during an existential crisis. When dating, we had liked the mind-bending movies. Stories within stories, inside someone's mind, like *Being John Malkovich, Adaptation,* and one of my favorites, *Eternal Sunshine of the Spotless Mind.* So, he tried to appeal to my analytical, deep side, as if I were capable of rational thought. He said something along the lines of, "If you are dead, why not make the best of it?"

For the record, if a friend asks you if they are dead, the correct answer is always an emphatic and reassuring "No."

It also didn't help that Rachel, the patient across the hall, screamed all night that *she* was dead. A mousy brunette in her early thirties, Rachel was in a collision when her vehicle crossed into oncoming traffic. Her mother told me Rachel underwent therapy while in a coma just to open her eyes. I now understand this type of "coma-stim therapy" involves repeated stimulation of the senses to help an individual become aware of his or her environment and awaken. At the time though, my confused brain envisioned a team of therapists working with her to physically open her eyes before she was ready. This, together with her nightly screams, left me convinced. She was the walking dead. Except she wasn't walking. She was in a wheelchair like me.

Rachel sustained frontal lobe damage, which meant she had drastic mood and personality changes. She alternated between sweet and hostile. Her yelling and name-calling became commonplace on the floor. She usually directed her anger at those trying to help her -- the nurses, her parents or husband. But she scared me. Then again, I was also afraid of the floor cleaner, a massive contraption pushed along with a thunderous and steady roar each night. Like many brain-injured patients, I was sensitive to noise. I thought it was chasing me. I could propel myself with my left foot by now and I always scurried in the opposite direction.

I couldn't seem to get away from the floor cleaner, but I could escape Rachel's screaming. I asked to be moved. I saw how unsettling the yelling was on the faces of my visitors. Scarier still, I was getting used to the insanity. Crying, calls for help, incoherent shrieks. Such was life on a brain-injury floor.

I moved from the Southside wing to a room on the Amelia Island wing. I viewed this just like the real-life neighborhoods the wings were named for. It was a step up. My mother was less enthu-siastic. My new room was one-third the size of my old one, and my mom said it felt claustrophobic. While I viewed my room as a cozy, safe haven, she encouraged me to get out, to take my meals in the dining hall.

There, a person could really crack up.

I said as much to Lisa, one of the assistants I befriended. Physically, I had things in common with other patients, but inside, I felt more like the staff. I became chummy with lots of nurses and their assistants (CNA's).

One evening I asked Lisa, as she alternated feeding me sporkfuls of turkey tetrazzini and overcooked vegetables (I had progressed to certain soft foods), "How do you not lose your mind?"

Surrounded by other patients, family members and staff, we sat at long tables in the dining room. Most of the patients wore robes or pajamas and those socks with the sticky feet. I was still in the pull-on sweatpants and matching hoodie they had dressed me in that morning for physical therapy. Not only did I believe in making an effort even in the hospital, but without my sneakers, I was immobile. The hospital footies didn't have enough traction to allow me to propel myself in the wheelchair.

Soft murmurs all around were punctuated by the occasional outburst. A thin Hispanic man sat diagonally from me, helped by his children. A girl, who looked to be seven or eight, buttoned up his robe, while her younger brother unrolled the silverware from his napkin. His wife sat close to him, speaking as if to a child, reminding him of various friends who'd asked about him. "Wasn't that nice?" she prompted with a weary smile. He stared at the silverware in his hand as if trying to remember what it was for.

Down at the other end, an old man cursed loudly. "Goddamn slop. Are we in prison here or what?"

At another table, an older woman cried softly. A nurse sitting with her encouraged her to take another bite. She shook her head. I wondered if it was the eating that was making her cry. Was she physically unable? Did she feel sick? Or was it something else?

"You're paying too much attention to it all," Lisa said. "Don't listen to any of it individually. You will go crazy. Just let it wash over you like background noise. Tune it out."

I should've listened to her. But I couldn't help zooming in on the scenes around me.

That's how I met Nokia.

Nokia was a kid from The Big Top pediatric wing. The Big Top housed everyone under 18, regardless of the type of injury, right alongside us brain-injured folks. Now Sunns is a top notch facility, but I've always wondered at the brilliant corporate mind that devised that plan. Was there no room on any other floor, next to the more benign injuries, like broken hips?

Nevertheless, there we were in the same room for lunch one day. Nokia reminded me of Gary Coleman on *Different Strokes*, the only other cute, mischievous, black kid I was familiar with. Nokia had been at Sunns numerous times, the latest stint to treat the burns from a fire at his foster home. A strange assortment of boys and girls of varying ages, kids you'd never see together under normal circumstances, surrounded Nokia. I sat alone, waiting for someone to come feed me.

People recovering from brain injuries often go through a period of behavioral changes. Hostility, like Rachel's, is common, but so is silliness. That was me. I laughed. A lot. Everything was funny. I'm talking, stitch in your side, pee in your pants funny.

Staff learned early on to take me to the gym down a back hall, so my howling laughter didn't cause a disruption among other patients.

At the top of every hour, the space in front of the physical therapy gym became a tangle of wheelchairs and attendants, all trying to get in or out. The first time I witnessed this traffic jam, I had just come down the elevator with whoever was pushing me. There must have been thirty wheelchairs all going nowhere. We couldn't even move out of the elevator for all the congestion. A busy rush hour. Someone kept holding the doors as they tried to bang closed. Nurses sighed and looked at their watches. Patients complained and shifted in their seats. Me? I'd never seen anything quite so amusing. Eventually, we rode back up so I could catch my breath and the nurses downstairs could get control of the situation. My laughter had been contagious.

Most of the time, however, something far more juvenile set me off. Anything "of the body" was hilarious. Burps, farts, boogers. The words poop and pee. I had the sense of humor of a 10-year-old boy. Nokia and I appealed to each other.

That day in the lunchroom, Nokia burped, and I laughed. So he did it again. And I laughed again. That's it. That's how it started. The friendship between children is so simple.

After that, I gave him the mini ceramic Christmas tree that my dad had given me. The twinkling lights and loud hum of electricity freaked me out. Nokia loved it and displayed it proudly, the star centerpiece among other donated decorations.

He came to my room, first in a wheelchair, then later as his scar tissue stretched, to show me he could walk again. He showed off his ability and I cheered for him. It only occurred to me later he didn't have family to say, "Watch me!" to. We were it. Me and some kids and the nurses. I wish I'd cheered longer.

Nokia came to my rescue the night Rachel cleared out the dining room. I found myself in there wearing pajamas and some socks with the sticky feet. One of my favorite CNA's, Natanya, had given me a bath and dressed me for bed before the early-bird dining hour of 4:30. She was trying to get a jump on her work. I didn't complain. I never complained.

I'd finished being fed when a nurse wheeled Rachel in. I heard her voice somewhere behind me, but never turned around. I didn't want to call attention to myself. I was on high alert. Every inch of skin on my backside pricked up. The back of my neck felt exposed and my shoulders hunched up.

"Take a bite," someone said.

"No," she spat back.

"You'd rather have this than a can, wouldn't you?"

I'd been threatened with the can before, a liquid supplement delivered by feeding tube. This worked on me. Not on Rachel.

"I don't care!" she hollered. Several people left the room.

"Look. It's macaroni and cheese You like macaroni and cheese."

"Ya'll are just bitches."

Several more groups hurried out. It was clear there was going to be a showdown. I was trapped. *Damn socks.*

"Rachel. You can't talk that way or you're going to have to leave. There are children in here."

Yes, I thought. *Please take her out.*

"Bitches!"

With that, a large group scampered out, trays in hand. Nokia and his posse of minors jumped up to my table in front of the room.

"We're outta here," he said.

"Don't leave me!" I pleaded.

Nokia sprang into action, ordering some teenager to grab my iced tea. Then he wheeled me out at a sprint all the way to my room.

We all arrived laughing and breathless. My adrenaline raced and my heart pounded as if I'd been the one running. It had been terrible and funny all at once.

I never said goodbye to Nokia. I'm glad. It would've been heart-breaking. I heard he cried the day he left. He didn't want to go to another foster home. Sunns was his home.

He left months before I did. Everyone did. People and seasons came and went. Only Rachel and I remained. It wasn't long before I had a new fear to focus on. I worried less about Rachel and floor cleaners. Instead, I wondered if I would ever get out.

CONSPIRACY THEORY

"You're still seeing that asshole?" Bob asked.

"Yeah," I said. I'm not sure why Bob thought the neuropsychologist at Sunns was an asshole, but I knew better than to get into it. Bob was a fellow patient on the brain injury floor and a person could get a lot more than he or she bargained for having conversations willy nilly. A simple comment about the peas at dinner could lead to a discussion about the habits of the farmer's pigs. Most people lived pretty far down the hall from reality.

I often saw Bob, his wife, Doris, pushing his wheelchair, on their evening stroll around the nurses' station. I took my own trek around the big loop that made up the second floor, wide hallways branching off at every wing.

The folks at Sunns had decorated the building in keeping with its name. Outside, it was painted a dark golden color, a deep mustard. Inside, it looked as if a canary had thrown up on everything. The halls, the rooms, the vinyl cushions of the dining chairs, all a pale yellow. I rolled by, looking at the cheesy motivational posters on the wall. They reminded me of my corporate days, but the slogans about perseverance and attitude had different meaning here. I rolled my eyes at one in particular. Hand drawn, there were birds and happy-headed flowers, all under a big, smiley-faced sun. The words 'Go The Extra Smile' were written at the bottom. The 'o' in 'Go' was another smiley face. Good grief. No wonder Bob was so cranky.

Winded, I veered crookedly down the hall, moving the wheelchair forward with my left arm and foot, keeping my right foot straight out in front of me to avoid the wheels. Still wearing an eye patch in a vain attempt to alleviate the double vision, I looked like some kind of deranged pirate, injured on the high seas.

Bob grumbled about something while Doris greeted me, prompting Bob with my name. "Hello there, Amy. See Bob? Amy *remembers*." Having memory there was like having stock options in Google. My mind was my ticket home. I just had to figure out a way.

My supervising doctor, a woman named Elizabeth Sweeney, assured me that Sunns wasn't a long-term care facility. I wasn't convinced. After all, I had been there almost three months already. Most everyone did a three-week stint. The only patient there longer was Rachel, and she was still name-calling and spewing profanity. I believed I had reached the only stop on my ride. I wasn't going home. They just hadn't found a way to tell me.

My case manager had written a discharge date of December 20th (the day after my 37th birthday) on the dry erase board in my room. That date came and went without mention. It became a joke. In the weeks that followed, nurses tried to erase it. In mocking defiance, I insisted they leave it there. I wanted everyone to see and ask me about it. It was proof they were lying to me.

Doris said they'd leave me to my appointment while Bob wished me luck with a sarcastic sneer. They disappeared down the hall just as I recognized the scuffed briefcase of Timothy Warren, M.D., Ph.D. approaching. It would be a few more weeks till I shared Bob's irritation with the doctor, though I'm sure it was for different reasons.

I guess it was some brand of psychology, to go along with me in my delusions, perhaps to gain my trust. Since I thought there was some massive conspiracy to keep me there, Dr. Warren played along, often darting into my room when we met there, as if being pursued. He acted the sleuth, ducking behind pillars so as not to be seen. I must have bought this early on in my self-deception. But he kept pretending long after I realized everyone there was trying to help me. Long after I knew there was no conspiracy. At that point, he just looked like an idiot.

It's no wonder I thought the way I did. My damaged brain tried to piece it all together, but the evidence was mounting.

Many patients were noted as "escape risks," due to their particular head trauma and subsequent mental state. They had I.D. tags attached to their wheelchairs that identified them as such, and an alarm sounded whenever they left the floor. I watched wide-eyed as a siren blared and one of the nurses at the desk shook her head laughing, then headed off to fetch the culprit. "Another one trying to escape," she said.

Also concerning was the mystery of the net beds. Years later, I learned that certain patients were in danger of waking up disoriented, forgetting they couldn't walk, and hopping out of bed in the middle of the night. For these individuals, there were net beds. I saw them across the hall, as some CNA tied large, see-through netting around them on their mattresses. It looked like some fantastical scene out of a sci-fi movie. I couldn't imagine what the contraptions were being used for, but it didn't look good. I needed to come up with a plan before they used one on me.

At least I one-upped them on the breathing machine. A respiratory therapist came to my room every few days or so, rolling in a large cart of equipment. The therapist hooked me up to a giant gadget with a mask that covered my nose and mouth. I later learned this device is called a nebulizer, and it delivers medication in the form of a mist directly to the lungs. Since I had contracted pneumonia twice already, it benefitted me to breathe in whatever antibiotics were being dispensed through this machine on wheels.

But I thought I was being drugged. And not in a good way. Thinking myself extremely clever, I adjusted the mask slightly and did my breathing out the side, avoiding most of the medication. The therapist would smile at me and go about the business of being a therapist, completely fooled.

My paranoia continued. I even banished my mother from the hospital for about three weeks. I wanted to get to know and observe people when their walls were down. I noticed the staff were on their best behavior whenever she was around. (True -- no delusion.) So I told her to stay away and "keep things on the down low," while I worked from the inside. Dr. Warren advised her to follow my instructions. I had obviously seen way too many spy thrillers.

Other characters in my drama were poor Mrs. Godfrey, tied to her wheelchair, whose brain was so damaged she kept trying to get up and walk; and the hostile man that stayed next door for awhile. He appeared well -- walked and talked just fine. But he'd been in a motorcycle accident and sustained a concussion. He fumed and cursed, insisting he was fine, demanding to be released, but an MRI showed tiny lesions on his brain. I know now, in cases of mild traumatic brain injuries like his, a person can appear injury-free, will not even recognize there's a problem, and become disabled a year later. At the time however, it was all more proof that something scandalous was occurring.

I also wondered at the large number of people in wheelchairs that I'd later see get up and walk. Why were they pretending to be worse off than they were? Even now, I forget that many people in wheelchairs *can* walk, just not for long distances. To this day, I stifle a little surprise whenever I see someone stand up from a wheelchair.

Given the craziness going on in my head, I did a fantastic job of appearing normal. Very few people knew my suspicions. A couple of doctors, some friends, and my mother. On the outside, I remained happy-go-lucky and made lots of friends. Inside, hospital life played out like a bad script.

In Dr. Warren's office that day, I pondered the fact that his window had yellow bars on it too, like the rest of Sunns, as if the psychologist himself was in danger of escaping.

"Yellow bars?" asked one of my former therapists, years later. "Oh, you mean the decorative crossbars on the building? I don't even know. I think that's paint."

Paint. I was chief detective starring in my own crime-thriller over yellow paint.

I've heard Rachel's been back to visit, walking with a cane. She doesn't remember much, least of all her violent outbursts, which she's deeply embarrassed about. I, on the other hand, never pass by Sunns and see those yellow bars without cringing.

MENTAL HISTORY

D r. Wacko's been Dr. Wacko to me for so long I've forgotten his real name. My mom and I nicknamed him shortly after he visited me in my hospital room.

He came at the invitation of my own doctor, Dr. Sweeney, who innocently asked if I would like to talk to someone. I agreed. In addition to crediting Dr. Wacko with ending my mother's banishment (while I investigated my conspiracy theory) it was from him I learned the distinction between psychologist and psychiatrist. The difference being Dr. Warren's mild form of talk therapy and the mind-numbing pills that Dr. Wacko dished out like free food samples at the grocery store. You could open a Walgreens with the array of mood modifiers he prescribed at first glisten of a tear.

I was in bed when he arrived (where else?) When you can't get up without calling a nurse, who then has to call a two-person lift team (two big black guys named Dwayne and Mike), you spend a lot of time between the sheets.

The fiftyish bearded man who entered was nothing like the flowing skirted, patchouli-wearing woman I had trusted with my innermost feelings a time or two before. This man looked like the professor of a dreaded subject, chemistry or trigonometry maybe. I no more wanted to share my troubles with this man than he wanted to hear them. Instead, he rattled off a series of questions.

"Do you have or have you ever had feelings of confusion?"

"Yes."

"Hopelessness?"

"Yes."

"Sadness?"

"Yes."

"Do you feel tired?"

"Yes."

"Have trouble getting out of bed?"

Here, I smirked.

Just then, my father and stepmother walked in. It was Friday afternoon. They usually came on the weekend. A once-a-month visitation. Not unlike my childhood. Also like childhood, I had the option of living with either parent when I was discharged. It was obvious I couldn't live alone (I was wearing adult diapers, for God's sake) and the hospital needed to know who'd be responsible for me.

I suppose I should've been grateful that both of them wanted me. That I was loved enough to have options. But, the choice paralyzed me, as much at 37 as it did at 10.

Just as no child should be made to choose between her parents, so too, should no brain-injured adult. True, I had suffered no cognitive brain damage. But, my faculties weren't quite on par. Picking a parent seemed an impossible thing for anyone to do, let alone someone who'd just undergone brain surgery. Still, I was an adult, and my parents had always treated me like one. They couldn't very well tell me what to do, could they?

Inexplicably, I chose my father. Wait, no, I can explain it. Much the same as in the emergency room, when I let Viv call my dad and not my mom, I think I was striving for normalcy. Never mind that my father lived in a completely different town, where I knew no one and where none of my friends lived. Never mind that there was no rehab hospital, no disabled community and handicapped services were close to non-existent. Never mind that my wheelchair didn't fit through a single doorway of my father's older ranch style house and he was facing a complete remodel.

Though I chose irrationally, deep down in the depths of my personality, I must have known that normalcy is overrated. I was having second thoughts.

"Oh good. You're here. You're the father?" Dr. Wacko asked.

Everyone introduced themselves. My heart beat faster. This was no good. I didn't even know this man. Or trust him. And what business did he have talking to my father?

After a little small talk, he returned to his interrogation. "Any history of mental illness in the family?" he asked my dad, not even looking at me.

History of mental illness? Did I hear that right? Who was this quack? Talking about me like I wasn't even in the room. I'm a coherent adult. Ask me!

And here, I couldn't believe it, my father paused. Paused like he was about to make a confession.

"Well, her mother's brother, I guess."

"What!?" I screamed, not caring how potentially nuts this could make me look. "Dad! Don't you realize what he's getting at?" I was flipping back the covers at this point. "That I'm crazy!" I yelled. I had to get out. I'd never been out of bed on my own before, but I didn't care.

My wheelchair was next to the bed and my sneakers were on it. I grabbed the sneakers in my good hand and half jumped, half fell into the wheelchair. My father made a grab at my elbow, but once I knew I had landed with success, I shrugged him off.

My socks slipped on the smooth linoleum as I clumsily propelled myself out of there, past all three speechless adults. I tried to slam the door, but lost my hold on it and it closed with a quiet click. I opened it back up and took another shot.

This time, the slam reverberated down the hall. Satisfied, I headed off, leaving them to talk about me and my mental state, but not before I put on my sneakers, laces trailing.

The episode upset me for several reasons, the first being that my father didn't know what he was talking about. My uncle was not crazy. Not certifiable. A little different, maybe. Eccentric.

He had never married, never had any girlfriends (or boyfriends) to speak of and had moved in with his mother, my grandmother, at thirty-something. He drove a 1976 Datsun until the parts started falling off on the highway. Magazines and newspapers were stacked so high in the little cinderblock home off of Miami's Flagler Drive, it resembled a set from an episode of *Hoarders*. And he still mowed the tiny patch of yard, surrounded by convenience stores and graffi-tied walls, with an antique push mower, whose ancient steel blades turned to cut the grass while he walked.

A little odd most would say. But he hadn't been diagnosed with any mental illness.

But that was my father. He was so polite to strangers, he would dredge up any old family weirdness just to be helpful. Like he didn't want the good doctor to go away empty-handed or stumped, so he came up with some tidbit he thought he remembered.

Another reason I was mad -- my father thought doctors were like the Secret Service running around with their walkie-talkies and earpieces. That "doctor's orders" were orders passed down directly from the President.

My mother, on the other hand, didn't have quite as much faith in the white coat. She allowed that a doctor was a person who'd gone through a bit more schooling and carried more letters after his or her name, but was a fallible human just the same. In her eyes, doctors often got it wrong, usually tripped up by their enormous egos.

But what bothered me most of all was that my father didn't know me, really *know* me, any more than Dr. Wacko. My dad had no idea if I was mentally sound or not.

When I finally returned to my room, Dr. Wacko had left and lunch had arrived. Dad and Deb fed me tuna salad and banana pudding, and no one uttered a word about what had just taken place.

That short consultation ending in disaster was all Dr. Wacko needed to set me up on an arsenal of medication. A doctor who had once filled in for Dr. Sweeney told me it was my right as a patient to know my medications. I began the next day, quizzing the nurses as to what each pill did before I swallowed it. I refused to take anything prescribed by Dr. Wacko. Mine became a dreaded room to have scheduled on the morning roster.

I heard later through a nurse that while I made life tougher for the nurses on the inside, my mom was giving them hell on the outside. She had requested copies of all my medications and was complaining all the way up the ladder to the Medical Director. I didn't know this at the time, just that she was out there walking the halls, catching this person or that going to lunch. Every nurse knew her and had made her copies.

I was being pushed back to my room after therapy one day when I heard my mom halfway down the hall. She had found Dr. Sweeney at the nurses' desk.

"I do *not* want him seeing my daughter again."

"Unfortunately, Ms. Quincy," Dr. Sweeney said, "that's not your call to make. Amy requested him. I'll need to discuss it with her if she wants to be taken off his list of patients."

"Take me off," I declared as the therapist rolled me to a stop behind them. "I don't want to see him anymore."

Dr. Sweeney looked at my mother and back. "Okay, if that's what *you* want," she said.

"It is."

We were a united front, my mother and I. Together in our positions, though we hadn't seen each other or spoken about it in more than three weeks. It's nice having her on my side.

EVERYTHING'S GOING TO BE OKAY

I was never baptized. I know, according to some faiths, this means I'm going to Hell, but I'm not too worried about it. I don't believe in Hell. I'm not sure what I believe in except this: there is, no, *has to be*, some method to this madness. It can't all be meaningless. I believe people are generally good, except for those who got messed up along the way and some random bad seeds of pure evil. But I don't think there is some hot, sweaty place where demons run around and those who spent their time on Earth being bad or not getting baptized are punished for all eternity.

I didn't grow up with any organized religion. Sundays were spent trying to "beat the church crowd," either at the Swensen's for brunch or out on the water in the boat. Dad hated both when it got too crowded and most of the "yahoos" out there couldn't be trusted behind the wheel of either boat or automobile.

This shortage of religion in my life is not a surprise considering my mother's family were Quakers, a group only surpassed in their lack of dogma by the self-described atheists and agnostics on my father's side. Atheist and agnostic seemed like dirty words until I looked them up. Agnostics don't deny the existence of a God, just that one can be proven. I can abide by that. Though, one look at the colorful variations of life on a coral reef, or anything in nature, is all the proof I need that a higher power exists.

Although my father's mother spent some time in a Catholic boarding school, she says they lost her when the nuns told her it was a sin to sew on Sundays, and that her mother wouldn't be allowed to join her in Heaven until every Sunday stitch was removed in Purgatory. My grandmother announced she was agnostic by the tenth grade. And there it is again. The defiance of any place not good. I come from a long line of eternal optimists.

Our faith, as a family, was tested during my near-death experience. I use the term near-death experience because Dr. Lewis operated just a hair shy of the many life-giving areas of my brain. Because I easily could have died. Not because my physical or spiritual body was actually close to death or I saw a white light of any kind. I didn't.

So while I was busy surviving nightmarish dreams and not seeing a white light, my mother was busy praying (hey, the 12 steps are firmly rooted in the belief of a higher power), and my father was busy crying. I learned all this about a month later, at Sunns Rehab, from good friends also present during the surgery.

"Hey, by the way," I said from my wheelchair during one of my dad and stepmother's visits to Sunns, "I'm really sorry for what happened back there in Gainesville. I guess I really scared everyone." I certainly had nothing to apologize for, but I still wasn't right in my swollen brain, nor would I be for close to a year. And it was my way, making sure everyone was happy and everything up front and out in the open.

"I always knew I was going to be okay," I continued, "but I guess you didn't."

Debbie nodded as if she understood perfectly. My father said nothing, but inside I knew he scoffed. I could practically hear his thoughts. *You were on a respirator with your head split open. What did you know?*

I have no idea why I said this with such confidence.

At Sunns, I was easy pickings for every religious fanatic that roamed the halls. Well, many of them were religious, only some, like Trisha, were fanatical.

A large number of patients were stroke survivors. Not hemor-rhagic strokes like mine, but ischemic strokes caused by a lack of blood to the brain, usually the result of a clot or blockage. There were wheelchairs everywhere and every manner of helmet and halo existed. Accident victims abounded. Many people had been with others who had died. It was a sad place.

Not surprising then, I stood out. I liked to laugh, make oth-ers laugh, and was generally upbeat. Plus, I remembered every-one's name.

This was unusual on a floor where patients often didn't know their own family members, let alone that Linda worked the gift shop. Though my memory was intact, it took awhile to prove to doctors I'd suffered no cognitive damage. While at Shands, I was repeatedly asked the year and the President's name. At Sunns, I was given word games and asked to repeat lists of items. I returned from one such memory test to find a woman about my age in my room.

"Hi. I'm Trisha."

She was a patient from another floor. She had short, blonde hair and wore casual athletic gear like most patients. And she was smart. She didn't get all preachy right away. That would have raised a red flag, even in my battered brain. She didn't ask if I'd been saved or anything like that. She just flattered me with talk about my positive spirit and how word of me had made its way to her. And before she left, she asked if we could pray. I nodded.

She knelt by my wheelchair, and I closed my eyes and bowed my head politely. As she spoke I heard the word Satan several times.

When she finished, I spoke in earnest. "I don't even believe in the devil."

"Of course, you don't," she said very matter-of-factly. "The light of our Savior has already filled you up."

It has?

I gave the matter some thought. Had I gone through some kind of God affirming spiritual awakening?

Most of my dreams, or hallucinations, since they followed me into the light of day, involved what I can only describe as some kind of spaceship. It was a big platform that people rode away on when they died to get another shot at life. Like we were all cats, but instead of nine lives, there was an infinity. It was as if I were playing a game, and if I lost I'd get some kind of massive do-over. Sometimes family members or friends were on the vessel, urging me to get on. I always tried. And failed. It was like trying to run away from the bad guy in a dream, only you seem to be frozen, unable to move. The spaceship always took off without me.

This did seem life-affirming, but I didn't think it could be called God affirming. I stayed on the lookout. I began to think maybe I had found God after John came into my room early one morning.

John, a sweet, older man with skin as dark as a walnut and a sparkly grin, worked nights. He'd seen me through the screaming nightmares and brought in his radio from home to play relaxing music when I couldn't sleep.

He and another aide came to take off the enormous plastic boot I slept in that was supposed to help keep my right foot from supinating and my ankle from spraining. It excelled at trapping my leg in the hospital bed rails and keeping me awake. When they freed me, the female aide said she'd stay to help me dress.

They greeted each other with familiar warmth.

"How are you today, Miss Theresa?"

"Blessed to be here, how 'bout you?"

"Mm-hmm," John murmured in low, guttural tones. "I know that's right. Gon' to be another glorious day!"

"Mm-hmm."

I looked back and forth between them as they worked over me.

"This one here, she understands," he said. I smiled, not really sure what he meant.

"Yeah?" Theresa looked me over with a new found respect.

"Sure. Jus' look a that smile." I kept grinning, wider now.

"Mm-hmm," she agreed.

"It's all over her. When people been through somthin', it happens," he said. "I see it all the time 'round here."

He would know. He saw it all the time.

I'm on a large boat. Someone is shooting. Strangers around me are dying, hit by bullets. I pretend to be dead. Bullets whiz around me. The shooting stops. I open an eye and see Danielle around the corner in another room, Frank just behind her. They motion me over. I have to get there. That is where it's safe. But I realize I can't feel my legs. I want to lunge over to where Danielle is, but I can't move. I'll never make it. I pretend to be dead again. The shooting starts back up. It's just a matter of time before I'm hit. Before I'm dead.

I hear a bird chirping. I'm saved. I don't know how or why, but I know everything will be okay. I don't know what the bird is saying, but this a signal I understand. It doesn't appear in my dream. It's on the peripheral, sounding in my ear. The bird chirps and I am flooded with relief. And peace. Everything is going to be okay. I am certain of it.

Next, the boat is gone. I'm walking across a field with Danielle and Frank's boys. It's dusk and the hills and tall grass are bathed in a golden glow, one tree in the distance. Nicholas and Max are running and playing up ahead. Michael is walking along with me, holding my hand. Another year and he won't do that anymore. He'll think he's too big to display affection. He's popping and smacking his gum, and I'm trying to get him to stop. He giggles.

Pop. Pop. Pop. Smack. Smack. Smack.

And then a little chirp. A bird twittering. More popping and smacking.

I stop walking and look down at him. "Did you do that?"

"Do what?" he asks, grinning.

We resume walking.

Pop. Pop. Pop. Chirp.

I stop again. He giggles, unable to contain himself. "It is! It's you!" I say.

He blows a big bubble and lets it pop. He pulls it off his nose, grins and giggles again. Then he shows me how he whistles just like a bird. I wake up.

It's been more than a year since the surgery and I'm at home on the phone with Danielle. Our conversation turns again, as it often does, to events of the past year.

"I told Michael about your dreams with the bird chirping," she says.

"Oh yeah? What'd he say?"

"He said, 'She must have heard my prayers, huh, Mom?'"

And you know what, Michael? I think I did.

MENTIONING
THE UNMENTIONABLES

No journey throughout hospital life would be complete without addressing the many complications involved in one of life's most private bodily functions -- going to the bathroom. Once a personal affair conducted behind a closed door, relieving myself now involved entire teams of people, written documentation, and a multitude of various locations and methods.

I am blessed to this day to have no knowledge of a catheter. One was used on me for at least the first month, but I remained horizontal and mostly in a fog. At Shands, physical therapists came in so I could practice sitting upright in a chair for ten minutes at a time. Usually, an alarm sounded indicating that my blood pressure had dropped and I would be returned to bed. There were so many tubes, carrying fluids both to and away from my body, that their purposes remained largely a mystery. At some point, it was decided that diapers would be the preferred method of waste disposal.

Since most people don't remember what it's like to wear a diaper, I'll tell you. It takes some getting used to. Going when you have to go, regardless of where you are or who's around can be a little awkward at first.

I did learn that the quickest way to clear a room of visitors was to call a nurse for a diaper change. Even the closest of friends suddenly had somewhere else to be. The only person this didn't work on was my mother. She remained undaunted by the diaper change.

In fact, I usually waited so long for a nurse to respond to the call button that my mom often took over the duty. This was always a mistake. She thought since she'd changed a diaper years ago, she still could. But she'd never diapered a 120-pound baby. By the time a nurse finally walked in, there I was, half-exposed in some gappy creation of my mother's, laughing while she cussed, the floor littered with botched attempts.

My mom was better with the bedpan. I was not. This required I master an opposite set of skills. Instead of becoming free enough to go whenever and wherever, the bedpan required me to go on command, within a tiny window of opportunity. After sensing the need, I would have to call for a bedpan, which might come right away or not at all. Then, if it was delivered and I still had to go, I had to pee with God knows who in the room, covered by only a bed sheet. The pressure to go was so great and I often suffered from stage fright. To avoid being unable to perform, I would wait till the last possible second to call for the bedpan. Then if it took too long, I would end up going in the diaper anyway.

I complained about this difficulty to a nurse, "It's like trying to pee in a bottle!" When that same nurse brought in a bottle one day after I'd called for a bedpan, I stared at her in horror. She assured me she was kidding. I hadn't gotten the joke, but everyone else had a good laugh.

It was tricky, this bedpan business. I never acquired this skill set during my stay. And if you couldn't prove you didn't need the diaper, you couldn't graduate to your big girl panties. I was discharged in diapers. At home, with no call button and no stage fright, I quickly became proficient in bedpan and advanced to real underwear within a month. Besides, by then it was only Nurse Quincy calling the shots, and she didn't want to be changing diapers any more than I wanted to be wearing them.

Simultaneous to the bedpan adventures, I also tried to get the hang of going on the toilet, like a regular person. This was challenging because it involved transferring and, therefore, called for even more people to be involved. (You try taking a dump with three people in the room and see how easy it is.) It's a wonder I went at all, but I was quite proud when I did.

A hospital isn't exactly the ideal setting for regularity. Like assembly line work, if you didn't produce every day, they wanted to know why. Staff got nervous on day two. Day three was Enema Day.

I lived in constant fear of the enema. And someone was always threatening to give me one. I wasn't worried about not going, but hospital staff could certainly get jazzed up about it. Heck, on vacation, I've waited entire long weekends before going. My mom doesn't think it's healthy, but I know my body, and I just prefer home.

The nurses kept track of all this information with detailed and precise recordings. I was surprised to hear medical professionals using the same discreet numbering system as the rest of the world. "Amy went number two in the toilet today!" one nurse would report to another with a clipboard. (Applause and cheers all around.)

One day, the nurse with the clipboard addressed me. "What did it look like?"

I thought I must have misunderstood. "Excuse me? *What did it look like?*"

"Yes, you know, size, shape, consistency. Anything."

The nurse who'd accompanied me shrugged. "I don't know. She flushed pretty quickly."

"I don't know," I said. "I didn't *look* at it." I hadn't realized there'd be a pop quiz on the subject.

"Next time, make sure you do," she chided me. "Remember, we need to know."

Once out of the hospital, my craving for privacy increased. People in wheelchairs, or anyone who has endured a long hospital stay, say they gave up any modesty they had a long time ago. Not me. Mine came back.

These days, I'm grateful I can shut a stall door behind me and go about my business in private. I take a much longer time, but don't worry, I still flush pretty quickly.

Part II: Recovery

PRETEND I'M NOT HERE

I'm lying face up on the tile floor of our patio. My mother's concerned face looms above me framed by the night sky. My cheek is throbbing. I wonder if my nose is bleeding.

"I'll go get some help," my mother says. "A neighbor ---"

"No!" I say. "I'm alright. We can do it." I've never been out of the wheelchair before. Well, I've been on the sofa, the bed. But on purpose. Not like this. This is foreign.

"Amy ---" she starts to protest.

"I'm okay. Am I bleeding?" I move my hand away from my nose and mouth for her to inspect.

"No, but let me go get some ice." She runs inside.

Bella blinks at me from the windowsill as if to say, *What the hell happened to you?*

She's what happened to me. She was tiptoeing past us into the night, and I lunged for her without thinking. I wasn't wearing the seatbelt that came on the wheelchair. I did a face plant into a potted palm. Bella scampered back inside the house. Rob had kept her and the kitten Ben while I was in the hospital. He adopted Ben and brought me back Bella. My mom had questioned my ability to handle two cats. Lying on the porch, I was beginning to see her point.

My mother puts a bag of frozen broccoli on my face. Everything hurts worse. Now I feel my knee, too. I look. Blood is winding its way down my bare leg. "Can you get something to dab at my knee?"

"Jesus, Amy. I think I should get some strong neighbor ---"

"No. Mom, please?"

"Well, how are we going to get you in?"

"Just wipe my knee. Let me think."

She disappears back into the house and returns with a dripping dishtowel.

After much discussion, we decide she should grab me by the ankles and pull me over the threshold. I want her to hurry before some neighbor walking the dog sees me out of the wheelchair and comes to investigate. I should be more worried about someone seeing my mother dragging what looks to be a dead body into the house.

It amazes me now, this predicament. I've fallen plenty over the years. Even intentionally falling out of the wheelchair onto a big, thick mat to do yoga. Now, I can scoot along the floor like a crab and haul myself up onto furniture. But then, I'd only been out of the hospital a couple months. This was April. I'd been discharged in February.

My mom spent all of March with the help of my friends, mainly Lee Anne, moving my belongings from the apartment where I did chair massage back out to the beach. She rented the downstairs unit of an old beach house for us. We asked the boys with their big TV to leave the house I owned. It was on the market. My mom handled everything. I never saw it again. It would've made me too sad.

Once inside the house, we contemplate how I'll get off the floor. First, I raise my butt a few inches. Mom stacks pillows under me, higher and higher, until I'm almost level with the couch. Then, she helps me transfer onto it.

The second time I fell was many months later. My mom and I had made new friends in the neighborhood, a lesbian couple named Kris and Lyn. Kris just happened to be a physical therapist who was now in insurance and worked from home. She took to working with me on her lunch hours, so I benefitted from our workouts long after I'd run through all conventional therapy. My health insurance only paid for therapy if I continued to improve at a certain rate. Kris believed there was still plenty of progress to be made. Though it was over time and on a smaller scale, improvement was still improvement.

As a result, I'd gotten stronger and was transferring in and out of the wheelchair on my own. I fell when I moved from a big, over-stuffed chair, lightly touched down on the wheelchair and kept right on going as it tipped over sideways. I laid sprawled across the living room floor, the wheelchair on its side, wheels spinning. My mother looked at me from her spot on the couch, a good deal less concerned than the first time.

"Okay, what are you going to do?" she asked.

"No, no. Don't get up," I said, waving my hand. "I've got it."

"Pretend I'm not here," she said.

Ah, the catchphrase. This would become my mother's go-to response (along with "it's good exercise for you"). She's an expert at providing "tough love" -- a term I swear she helped coin. My mom uses one of these two phrases each and every time any normal person might feel compelled to take action or provide assistance.

Like in my aunt's pool later that spring, I splashed around in the shallow end without a flotation device, seeing what I could do. I was trying to hold on to the edge and kick my legs out behind me. As usual, I lost my grip on the right side. I faltered a minute trying to get my footing. I went under.

I came up laughing. "I'm okay! I'm okay!" I said, for the benefit of my family. My mother was in the pool, my aunt stood at the edge and my grandmother sat nearby in a lounger. My laughter had caused me to take in some water and I started coughing. I went under again, tried to place my feet on the bottom.

The next time I came up I heard my aunt shouting to my mother, "*Suzanne!*" After some more sputtering and floundering, I was able to push my head out of the water. My mother stood all of a foot away. First she chastised me, telling me my laughter would be the death of me. Then, to my worried aunt and grandma, she extolled the importance of allowing me the time to learn.

I have to say I agree. Later, I would take an adaptive swim class with other disabled people at a local gym. I could never experiment with my abilities enough. Everyone was always worried about me. Granted, there was liability to consider and I did splash and flail about like a drowning person. I was certain some lifeguard was going to jump in and try to save me. They probably drew straws to see who got stuck with the handicapped class.

My ataxia is to blame for my lack of coordination. Damage done to my cerebellum, either by the bleed or the surgery that saved my life, left me with this movement disorder. There is no cure for ataxia, and medicine does little to help, particularly in my case. Understanding my herky-jerky nature is like getting a refresher course in anatomy and physiology. I learned that skeletal muscles come in pairs. The undamaged brain sends a signal, and both muscles move simultaneously, producing one fluid movement. In simplest terms, my brain misfires. The two muscles work independently of each other. Their timing is off. As a result, I'm more likely to punch myself in the eye than scratch my nose. The ataxia is much worse on my right side, so I'm more likely to use my left.

It affects every muscle in my body, including my abs, so even my sitting balance can be iffy. Which is why I'd rather stay in the wheelchair at a restaurant than transfer to a booth. Of course, my mother loves the booths, as I did before getting there became a big production, so I often transfer.

At a Denny's one busy morning, I transferred over to the booth and failed to stop the forward momentum of my body. Like a weeble-wobble, my torso laid all the way down on the red vinyl for a quick moment before popping back up. My mother looked at me, suppressing a laugh, like she just heard a loud fart at a cocktail party. It's wildly inappropriate, but funny, too. Her eyebrows shot up and she looked amused. "Well!" she said. We laughed.

We often have more fun than anyone around us. We're usually getting a good chuckle out of my spastic antics, while others look on, unsure whether to join in the laughter or offer assistance.

One evening, my mom came home to find me in the bathtub. I think she was as proud of me as I was. It was just like old times. Enya blasted from the living room speakers and the bathroom was dimly lit by a night light, which I'd decided would have to do in place of candles. I relaxed in steaming hot water. Bubbles were everywhere. She said hello and left me alone.

The problem arose after I dried myself and put my tennis shoes on. (Funny is a naked woman in sneakers.) As I attempted to pull myself out of the tub, the floor-to-ceiling pole I use came out of the ceiling. I landed out of the tub, but nowhere near my wheelchair, sitting on the cool tile surrounded by bits of drywall. The pole hung across the toilet and sink, still firmly connected at the base.

"Mom!" I called. To her credit, she didn't utter the catchphrase. I suppose I could have scooted my naked, clean body and my wheelchair all the way into the living room and across the hardwood floors to climb on the couch. I *could* have if I had to. She held the wheelchair and helped me into it. I could pretend she's not here, but it's nice that she is.

I'D RATHER BE BLIND

A few months out of the hospital and I was fat. Well, not *fat* fat. But fat for me. A size 8, size 6 if really working at it, I now fit comfortably in a 12. That meant my mom bought me 14's and 16's.

Having never forgotten her days of dressing me, she thought everything should slide up and on with nary a tug. Everyone knows jeans don't fit that way. But jeans were a thing of the past living under her roof. So was anything with zippers or buttons that she'd have to help me fasten. Everything in my closet now came two sizes too big with an elastic waist. She once brought home a six-pack of Hanes panties that were so huge I couldn't tell the front from the back. Such is your fate when you can't do your own shopping.

So, unable to wear her purchases without looking like an 80-year-old convalescent, I was determined to fit into some of my old clothes. Trouble was, Mom was also doing the grocery shopping.

I love food. I find it to be one of the great joys of living. In the hypothetical game of "which you'd prefer to lose," your sense of taste or your sight, I'd rather be blind. My mom thinks that's nuts and says she'd much prefer to lose flavor. That's assuming, she says, she's still *able* to eat. And I guess I should be more specific. Because being hooked up to a feeding tube is pretty grim.

I ate that way for months in the hospital while attending speech therapy classes to learn how to eat without choking. I took barium tests at the hospital swallow clinic. The x-ray technician analyzed the actions of my esophagus while I drank metallic liquid through a straw.

Each day, I came back to my room after various therapies to be hooked up, via the port in my stomach, to a bag of thick, yellow liquid. It looked like fat. There were cans of the stuff stacked up in my room. Long after I started eating soft foods, the nurses would threaten me with the supplement.

"You should put more bananas on your menu. You need the potassium. If we don't get those numbers up, we'll have to give you a can."

The nurses lived by the numbers, which they knew because they woke me every so often at 5:00 a.m., so an orderly could take a vial of my blood.

There was real cause for celebration when I graduated from the sack of fat to pureed food. My first pureed meal was beef with a side of broccoli, fed to me by the usual gang of friends. They laughed at me enjoying my plate of mush. The green mound was shaped like a little floret, lest there be any doubt as to its identity. I was in heaven at the taste -- exactly like broccoli.

A little while later, I advanced a level. Now I could have those foods the healthcare system calls "mechanical soft." Nurses fed me, due to the ataxia. I had been there sufficient time and befriended enough staff to know what they called me. I was a "feeder."

I heard the aides talking to one another. "When do you get off?"

"I've got two more feeders, then I'm done."

Mechanical soft food was what you might expect: egg salad sandwiches, macaroni and cheese and creamed corn. I had crustless sweet potato pie at Christmas. I chose mashed potatoes and gravy with everything. Hey, I had weight to gain.

Nurses removed the trach by the end of 2006. The hole at the hollow of my throat would close on its own. A piece of gauze was placed there with some surgical tape. I worried obsessively about it when I ate.

"Is food coming out?" I asked the CNA, Natanya.

She laughed at me. "If food was coming out, you'd be choking, not talking."

It was no longer necessary to put thickeners in my drinks, but I would always have to drink through a straw. The feeding tube was the last thing to go, removed just weeks before I left the hospital February 18, 2007. I weighed 128 pounds. At almost five-foot-nine, I was too skinny.

I didn't realize being in a wheelchair and on the downside of 35 would drastically affect my weight. In hindsight, I should have gained about ten pounds. Instead, I embarked on a happy-to-be-alive free for all.

My mother's food philosophy didn't help much. She thinks the concepts of reduced fat and fat-free are scams. Her motto is, "If you're going to do something, do it right." She goes for full-on fat. And, as I said, she was the one doing the grocery shopping.

She brought home blueberry pies and Stouffer's Fettucini Alfredo from Publix. We had the little chocolate covered ice cream treats called Dibs for dessert. One of the first times she left me alone, I was so thrilled, I went straight for the Dibs as soon as her car pulled out of the driveway. An often overlooked benefit of feeding yourself is being able to eat whenever the mood strikes.

My mom came home to find me in the living room covered in chocolate.

"It's pretty bad in there," I warned, as she approached the kitchen.

Bad was an understatement. It was a Dibs massacre. Little pools of melted ice cream lay all over the floor, where they'd landed when I tried to open the container. I'd attempted to clean up, tossing them into the sink, before remembering I could no longer throw with any accuracy. A few had made it in, but most were splattered against the back wall and toaster. Finally, realizing I was only making matters worse, I backed out of the galley-style kitchen, crunching over candy-coated shells as I went.

My mom surveyed the scene.

"What *happened?*"

After that, we switched to ice cream sandwiches.

At that point, my main concern wasn't what to eat, it was *how* to eat.

Having the use of only one shaky hand decreases the chances of food making it to your mouth. And yet, I gained. My mom and some friends still fed me most times. And always at restaurants. I used to love going out to eat, but I was revising my opinion.

I hate being fed, particularly in public, sitting there like a dope with a straw in my wine glass. I've learned to order a mixed drink, or if I really feel like wine, a different glass.

Soon I realized I could feed myself if I chose what I ate. This realization came none too soon. I was tipping the scales at 183.

I'm back down to 150 now and trying to lose the last ten, like most women I know. I never fit into most of those old clothes. They were too sexy for a woman in a wheelchair approaching 40.

Physically, I can eat anything I want, though I'm likely to cough and sputter over nuts, carrots, or popcorn. I still like going to restaurants. I'll let myself be fed if I'm hungry and it's difficult fare. Recently, a waiter asked if my mom and I would like to hear about the desserts.

"Always," I replied.

They had a lovely homemade peanut butter pie with crushed Reese's topping drizzled with warm chocolate sauce.

Well, maybe just a life-is-good sliver.

RIDING THE SHORT BUS

In July 2007, I began riding Connexion. That's Jacksonville Transportation Authority's door-to-door service for those unable to ride the regular city bus due to a disability. In short, the short bus.

I found out about it from Johnny at outpatient rehab, where I went twice a week. Johnny looked to be in his sixties, with faint wrinkles over tanned skin and a crew cut. He was retired and had suffered a stroke. He cruised around the gym in his wheelchair with his cane and coffee cup, befriending everyone, including me.

I learned a lot from Johnny. He was the first person I met who got around like me, propelling his wheelchair with his feet. He only used one hand too, which I later realized was a sure sign of a stroke. He kept his cane attached to his chair, though I'd never seen him walk with it, and his bus fare on the ready in a fanny pack. He found it easier than fumbling one-handed through a wallet. He showed me how his dollar bills were folded into crisp squares around his quarters. The bus took exact change only. I wondered at all those sharp creases and if his wife helped him.

Johnny and I used to bet on whose ride would arrive first. Back then, I was still taking a van from Advanced Patient Transportation that outpatient rehab paid for. I always won. Poor Johnny was forever waiting on JTA, but I envied him his freedom.

So I memorized the number on the side of the bus, and by summer I was waiting on them too. They would take me anywhere in the city for $2.25, as long as I arranged it the day before.

The first day I took the bus, I was half an hour early, which ended up being an hour and a half early. They schedule half-hour pick up windows, during which time you have to be ready to go. So if you want them at 9:00, your pick up window is 8:30 to 9:00. If you're early on top of that and they're late, well... you get the picture. It's a lot of waiting around.

I was outside and ready to go when a neighbor drove by in her car. She slowed down and shouted to me out her window, "Hi, neighbor! I'm Lucy."

She'd seen me at a garage sale two blocks over held by a woman named Michele. Michele held the sale to raise money for an item I still get great use out of -- a beach wheelchair that travels over soft sand. Lucy, Michele and I became good friends. They were the first friends I made as a disabled person. The first friends that didn't know the old me. I was beginning to realize that person might be gone forever.

After Lucy leaves, the bus arrives. My ride to wherever I'm going that day is uneventful. I go straight there. As I soon learn, this is a rarity.

On the way home, I notice the driver's sour disposition. After my wheelchair is locked down, I hand her the fare from my fanny pack. I had balled up my dollar bills around my quarters. Inside I smile, imagining my mother's expression if I'd asked her to fold my ones. I apologize for my crumpled money. The driver grunts at me.

Unfamiliar with the system, I inform the driver on every wrong turn she takes away from my house. I figure she is confused. We aren't even heading east.

After my third helpful suggestion, the driver not so patiently informs me she is picking up other passengers. I flush hot, shut my mouth and arrive home two hours later.

I've since learned that there's a rule that no one should be on a bus more than 90 minutes. What if you have to go to the bathroom? Or you're diabetic? Someone must have thought of these things. After all, this little bus is not transporting the healthiest people in the world.

On board, I travel with all nature of illness. From people attached to wheeled tanks of oxygen, to the gray, thin-skinned bodies of the elderly on their way home from dialysis. There are old men in pajamas and socks headed to medical buildings with caregiver escorts that didn't even bother to dress them. These people never say a word, just sit in lifeless heaps in their blanketed wheelchairs while the drivers move them to and fro, their heads lolling about as if sleeping.

The sick are always quiet. Not so with the disabled, particularly the mentally challenged. A girl once told me she had a 30 pound service cat trained to alert her of an oncoming seizure. Now I believe animals can sense things way beyond our detection. But 30 pounds? I've never even heard of a service cat, let alone a fat one.

Another woman shrieked diabolically every time we went over a bump. I could only guess she was in some kind of pain. The driver kept apologizing and creeping along at 15 m.p.h. She was so distracted by the screams, she took a wrong turn into an apartment complex that was nothing but speed bumps. Always eventful.

And the neighborhoods. I've seen sides of Jacksonville I never even knew existed. Beautiful homes surrounded by dripping Spanish moss tucked along the St. Johns River. A nurse or middle-aged child stands in the driveway of these houses waiting to collect an aging parent, while in another part of town, an old woman relies on the driver to escort her to her door as she pushes her walker in tiny, shuffling steps.

At times, I've felt like the only light-skinned person for miles around. We've driven through government housing projects, full clotheslines flapping in the breeze, while entire families sat on the stoop, watching us pass. I always hope that whoever we pick up from these concrete boxes isn't on board when we reach my house. Then, I'm the little rich girl. If the driver pulls far enough down my street before turning around, we will see the ocean. My beach wheelchair sits on the front porch. I'm only grateful that my third wheelchair, the motorized one Kris found for me through her physical therapy contacts, is inside. Both were donations, but still.

And yet, with all I have, I long for the dingy apartment across town I watched that woman slowly shuffle towards. Well, maybe not *that* apartment but one like it. On the first floor with a ramp and a handrail leading to it. I knew it was all accessible inside, too, because there were two peepholes. One at regular eye level and one lower, at wheelchair level. I bet the microwave is on the counter instead of built in five feet high. I love living at the beach, but it's not exactly land of the accessible apartments.

My mom rented this one, then the one above it, in a pinch. She decorated. Sure, it was with my stuff, and she consulted me, but it's not the same. Riley kept reminding her not to use area rugs. I know she can't stand it. She keeps sneaking a little rug in at the base of the kitchen sink. It gets rumpled up and in my way until I whip it out of there. She finds it in a heap at the entrance to the galley kitchen. It's our unspoken stand off. Or more likely, I'm standing off, and she's just clueless.

Riding the bus, seeing how other people live, I'm sure of it. I want a real place of my own.

One evening, I am on my way home from the outpatient gym. I've fallen into a bad habit since the hemorrhage. Or maybe it's not so much bad habit as it is human nature. I've been comparing. I see lots of disabilities now and I decide in my head if someone is better or worse off than me. It's terrible I know, but it's what I do. Amputee? Better off. Prostheses are amazing now. Mentally challenged but can walk? Worse off. I don't think I'd trade my mind for any physical ability. Paraplegics are a toss-up. It depends on the level of injury.

A blind woman is already on the bus when I'm picked up. I realize she's blind when I say hello and she responds in my general direction, but seems to make eye contact with my left shoulder. Her eyes look layered over with coke bottle glass.

Next, we pick up a woman coming from work. She has dwarfism. I believe the politically correct statement is that she is a little person. She couldn't be much over three feet tall, and she's lugging a suitcase on wheels. Her pudgy fingers are wrapped around a handle, that if extended, would be well over her head. I watch her begin the laborious climb up the three steps of the bus. She heaves the bag up one step and rests her hands on top of it while she positions her feet on the step below. The driver offers to help, but she declines. I steal a glance as she buckles her seat belt. Her legs extend straight across the seat, her feet barely dangle over it. On occasion, I run across things I can't reach or a car blocking my access to a curb. It pisses me off when well-meaning people put stuff in the very back of the freezer. Or on a high shelf in the kitchen or on top of the fridge. Or any other of the multitude of places I can't get to. But that's only on occasion. Her entire world is oversized.

Our motley crew continues down Beach Boulevard. At a stoplight, I hear music coming from a Ford Explorer in the next lane. A blonde has the window rolled down and her elbow out, resting on her knee. I used to drive like that. One foot tucked up under me.

The blonde turns to look at the bus, and I feel grateful for the tinted windows. I used to look at the short busses, too, the blue handicapped symbol on the back, and wonder about the poor souls on board. Now I'm on the inside.

The sunset is so spectacular that evening that I'm sure it'd warrant comment by the driver or passengers if one of those passengers wasn't a blind woman. So instead, we all sit respectfully silent in the warm glow of pinks and reds. I watch as the blind woman adeptly handles her cell phone to call a friend, then a Chinese takeout place, something I can never do without misdialing or dropping the phone altogether. Then I listen as she inquires about the specials and places her order. This is also something I cannot do, as I'm hard to understand and often misunderstood or hung up on like a prank caller. I think about her eating her fried rice, something I avoid because it falls off the fork. Then, I turn in time to see the last of the pink sun sink beneath the horizon. I think about comparisons and how I said I'd rather lose sight than taste, and you know what? I take it back.

PERSPECTIVE

The opening scene is shot from the point of view of a man in a hospital bed. A gentleman in a white coat goes from clear to blurry as the man whose eyes we are looking through wakes up. The doctor explains, "You're in a hospital...you've had a stroke...you were in a coma for almost three weeks, but now you're waking up and you'll be fine." Later he instructs, "Now try saying your name."

Jean-Dominique Bauby. We hear a second voice in French and the subtitled words flash on the screen.

"Go on, try," says the doctor.

I just did.

"Try hard! Tell me your name."

Jean-Dominique Bauby.

"Try to say your children's names."

Theophile, Celeste, Hortense.

"Don't worry. It's a very slow process. But your speech will come back."

What? Can't you hear me? Doctor!

We are left with only one voice as the doctor moves away. It becomes clear his was the only voice to speak aloud. We continue to hear Bauby's thoughts. *What's going on? I can't speak? They can't hear me. My God!*

This is how the French film *The Diving Bell and the Butterfly* opens. At times, the audience sees only what Bauby sees. And he can't move or speak. He's paralyzed from head to toe. The film follows the true life story of Jean-Dominique Bauby, age 42, as he lives with "locked-in syndrome," able only to blink and communicate with his left eyelid. I get claustrophobic just looking at it. This is what being buried alive must feel like.

The film came out in 2007 and received four Academy Awards in 2008. Bauby dictated the book the film was based on, using a communication system devised by his speech therapist. In it, the alphabet was read in order of frequency of use, with Bauby blinking to indicate the correct letter. Sometimes, I feel sorry for myself, slowly pecking away at my keyboard with just thumb and index finger. Bauby dictated an entire book by blinking, letter by painstaking letter. I think of him often.

A friend gave me a copy of the film on CD before it came out on DVD. It must have been a pirated copy. In principle, I don't like that. I think movies, like books, are pieces of art made by artists. It's like taking the ramen noodles straight from some starving artist's mouth. I won't watch a pirated copy. Except *The Diving Bell and the Butterfly*.

I was just out of the hospital -- I wasn't yet standing on my own principles. Just like I ate meat while at Sunns. I was fortunate enough I could eat. I wasn't going to be particular about what was on the menu.

The day I was discharged, I switched back. That final lunch, I turned down the chicken salad, to the surprise of all the nurses.

"You should have said something!"

"We could have brought you vegetarian meals!"

Bauby ate through a tube. Like me, those first few months. But I got off the tube; Bauby never did. The thing I found unexpected, was there were no cravings. I never felt hungry. I realize now, most of the enjoyment of eating comes from satisfying your hunger. I spend a good portion of my day just thinking about my next meal. Deciding what I'm hungry for and then eating it. It's so simple. Something most people do every day without thinking about it. I think about it now.

The only fortunate thing, if anything in Bauby's situation can be called fortunate, is that the hospital was right on the ocean. A naval hospital on the coast of the French Channel, Berck-sur-Mer is where Bauby spends his days in Room 119. He is frequently wheeled to a large balcony in the open air to take in the view of the sea and the Berck-sur-Mer lighthouse. His children and their mother often visit with him on the beach, the children frolicking in the sand.

One of the most beautiful, telling shots in the film is of Bauby, utterly alone and bundled in his wheelchair, on a dock that is suspended over breaking waves.

Bauby died just two days after his memoir was published. Like me, Bauby suffered a rare stroke in the brain stem. He was only a few years older than I was when it happened. He died of pneumonia. I had pneumonia twice. Sometimes, the only difference between living and dying is wanting it so.

MAKE BEAUTY

I lay face-up on the table clenching my fists while the smell of burning hair fills the room. *Zap zap zap!* Hair sizzles as the light from Alexandra's laser gun flashes. We both wear big plastic goggles to protect our eyes. *Zap zap zap!*

"You du-zing okay?" she asks.

There is something fitting about having your unwanted hair removed by someone with a thick Russian accent.

"Fine," I reply.

I'm not lying. The multiple procedures are worth any amount of pain and money. Anything to avoid the humiliation of last month's trip to the pool with hairy armpits.

I wasn't real hairy, or I would have stayed home, but I had enough to make me self-conscious. In my former life, when I could shave myself, I wouldn't dream of leaving the house in a sleeveless top without freshly shaven underarms, or going to the beach without giving my bikini line the once over with a disposable Bic. Now spaghetti straps are a thing of the past, and my dresser houses at least two pairs of boy shorts. Boy shorts are a must for the wild woman. And, much to my dismay, I have become a wild woman.

Happily, I've found a solution to tame me. My mother thinks it's ridiculous to pay good money for someone to inflict pain. But she'll come around when she's not shaving my underarms and bikini line all the time. She says she doesn't mind, but the truth is, she really doesn't do a good job.

She used to shave my legs, too, until I got tired of catching glimpses of my own hairy ankles. Now I get them waxed, along with my eyebrows, at the Vietnamese nail salon near my house.

They love me there. They should. I'm in there every two weeks. I get my nails manicured and alternate between leg waxing and pedicures.

"Must be nice, " people say to me. Or, "Well, la-di-da."

I could respond that it must be nice to be able to file your own nails, but I don't. It's not that I'm a princess. I just can't do these things myself, and good grooming's important to me. So sue me.

I confess, I'm no stranger to the mani-pedi. They knew me at the salon before the hemorrhage, back when I climbed into the pedicure chair instead of being hoisted into it by one person under my arms and one under my legs. I tried explaining that I could stand, but no one speaks very good English, and I don't think they knew what I was talking about. Now I just let them lift me. I'm lucky if I'm able to communicate enough to get the wheelchair brakes set. Last time, they scooped me up before I'd locked them and the wheelchair went rolling across the salon.

I'm sure it's quite a sight for other customers. There are four or five technicians in a circle around me, shouting instructions to each other in Vietnamese. I've learned to just shut up and be still. They'll handle everything.

I'm treated a bit differently by people from this country. Americans are more concerned with liability. I do my aquatic exercises with two life belts on. The instructor isn't allowed in the pool unless I'm drowning, which would be quite a feat engulfed by yellow plastic in three feet of water.

Zap zap zap! Alexandra moves on to the nether regions.

Yow. This hurts more than usual. Did my mom not apply enough numbing cream?

"You needz more of zee cream here." *Zap zap zap!*

Okay. I'm going to kill my mother.

"Be liberal with that stuff," I'd told her earlier that morning. She was late, as usual, and I panicked when I heard her groggy voice on the other end of the line. Calling her on the phone instead of down the hall was a new arrangement. Sometime late that summer she'd rented the apartment above the one we had shared. I was now alone downstairs. It gave us both some much needed breathing space.

"Where *are* you? The cream! It has to be on for two hours to work!"

"Huh?"

"The *numbing* cream. My appointment. Just get down here. Don't even brush your teeth!"

She dabbed it on quickly and covered it, per the instructions from the office, with Saran Wrap. Now when anyone needs to cover food, I direct them to the trunk in my bedroom.

"Right," said my friend Rhonda the other day, "because that's where I keep it."

My mother hates the cream process, as she hates all directions with more than three steps. I had foolishly placed the scissors on my nightstand, anticipating neat little strips of Saran Wrap cut to cover each area. Next to the unused scissors was the unused masking tape. As she ripped and tore plastic from the roll, she decided my underwear could hold the cling wrap in place.

I lay there, spread eagle on my bed while my mother fought with the sticky stuff attaching and folding up on itself. Then she helped me slide up my underwear.

"Careful. No. You hold the plastic while I pull them up," I instructed.

"I *am*."

"No, you're not. That plastic is getting all messed up. Here. Let go."

"Jesus, Amy."

When we were done, I felt like I was wearing a diaper. It crinkled whenever I moved.

And now, I'm not even numb. It had all been for nothing.

When the zapping stops, I ask Alexandra to explain to my mother how much cream is needed. Coming from me, it will just sound like criticism.

"It needz to be very thick. Like ice-zing zee cake."

My mother nods and reaches for my hand. She feels terrible.

The next day, my crotch and underarms are still sore. My friend, Pat, picks me up for the trip to the nail salon and sees me wince.

"Unmedicated assault with a laser gun," I say.

Later in the car, Pat says, "I think I might stay and get a pedicure."

This is huge. Usually she just drops me off and runs errands. But she is slowly coming around. Two weeks ago she had her eyebrows waxed. And this will be her first pedicure. Ever.

"I'm just thinking about it," she says. "I feel bad, though. Like I should take that money and give it to charity or something."

"Do both if you can afford it," I say. "I do."

"You do?"

I nod. This seems to make her feel better. So when we enter, I announce that she wants a pedicure. Someone immediately ushers her to a pedicure chair.

I hear her hemming and hawing, but the salon workers take over. It's futile to resist.

"Why not? Why not? Feel good. You relax," they command in their broken English.

It is hard to argue. Why not feel good? Yes, indeed.

"Oh, pamper yourself a little," I say. "Besides," taking the opposite approach, "it's not how good you feel, it's how good you look."

Okay, so maybe I am a little bit of a princess.

A woman massages my right arm and hand. "Feel good?" she asks. I imagine it must though it only feels tingly, like when a limb falls asleep. I nod and smile at her, skipping *that* conversation.

After Pat's pedicure and my manicure, we sit in the waxing room. She watches as two women pull strips from my legs. For some reason, the main woman who does this can't seem to resist holding up a gummy strip to show me all the hair that formally resided on my body. She loves this and does it without fail. Maybe it's job security. Proof that I'd be a wooly mammoth without her. It works.

Now that my legs are smooth, it's Pat's turn. She lies back on the table while someone helps me with my socks and shoes.

"I know. I know," she says. I turn around to see a sticky eyebrow strip being held up to her face for inspection.

"Make you beauty," the wax woman, Lee, says. "Get you husband."

"She already has a husband," I offer.

"Make husband love you more," she says.

Pat raises one perfectly arched eyebrow at me from the table and I smirk. Lee applies wax to her other brow with a toothpick.

"You know, Frida Kahlo left her facial hair alone," Pat said, referring to the famous uni-browed artist.

I visualize Salma Hayek who played her in the movie *Frida*. "No offense," I say, "but we're not that beautiful."

There is a moment of silence and then, "Nooooo."

When I look, Pat has wax applied to one side of her upper lip. Lee reaches for a strip. Pat's eyes are wide. She only wanted her eyebrows done.

"For free. For free. Make beauty," Lee says.

Lee is a perfectionist. I love her for that. I let her wax my whole face. It started out with just my eyebrows and extended last month, horror of horrors, to my chin. Don't you know she showed me the used strip with the rogue chin hairs to prove it?

We overtip and leave with angry red marks on our faces. Pat emails me later that evening to say her husband looked right at her and didn't notice a thing.

What can I say? He *is* a man.

I email her back that he most certainly will love her more. He won't have any idea why, but he will. "Besides," I write, "you look fabulous."

And after all, it's not how good you feel, it's how good you look.

TRAVELS WITH MOM

As the anniversary of my hemorrhage approached, I thought about ways I could commemorate it. I wanted to do something grand. I wanted to celebrate my life and the fact that I still had a place in this world. I wanted to prove I was still the independent, high-spirited girl who had biked through Europe. I wanted to travel.

I'd always had "the bug." Now that the crisis was over, it returned. I knew I'd never again traverse the globe alone, so I decided solo travel wasn't the holy grail I'd thought it was. I remembered lonely nights spent huddled in my tent while the rain beat down. I remembered picturesque vistas with the twinge of sadness that accompanied them because I had no one to share them with. And I remembered the worst element of all - the table for one.

So I began planning a mother-daughter trip for Mom's birthday in September. I chose Seattle and the San Juan Islands. Off the coast of Seattle's Puget Sound, the San Juan Islands boast tremendous wildlife viewing opportunities, including the likelihood of seeing Orca whales.

Half the fun of any trip is in the planning, and I had a blast. I enjoyed the unique challenge of planning handicapped travel. I hadn't flown in years, and never in a wheelchair, and I reveled in my to-do lists. I had my quart-sized baggies and three-ounce containers ready to go one month out. I decided to take the power chair so Mom wouldn't have to push me. It could lug my heavy duffel bag, the only bag I would take, looped over the head rest. I checked with the airline to confirm there would be a narrow "aisle chair" to get me to my seat, and I booked handicapped rooms. I delighted in being understood. I rented a wheelchair van that Mom could drive. It had a ramp that slid out automatically after the side door opened. A nice gentleman named Steve informed me the passenger seat would be removed at no extra charge, so I could roll right in. I was thrilled at the ease with which I could operate with the right, albeit expensive, equipment.

As the trip took shape, I got more and more revved up. I could still travel! I set future trips: Ireland with Lucy and the Grand Canyon with Michele. My mother bragged to her friends how I planned everything. Mom isn't a planner. "Just tell me where to be," she joked, as I organized the trip, occasionally asking for her credit card or driver's license.

I had romantic notions of mother and daughter, having weathered hard times, bonding together over this new undertaking. I envisioned us laughing over some incident while we took in the Seattle skyline from the waterfront, enjoying the city's fresh seafood and Starbucks. I imagined us on a crag of rocky coastline, watching an Orca and her calf, blowing sprays of cold Pacific water that gently misted over us.

Reality interfered.

"Shit," my mother said as she stalked off the elevator of Sea-Tac International.

"Mo-om!" I hollered. The elevator doors started closing behind her, leaving me, too slow to exit, still on the elevator.

"Shit," I heard her say again. As the doors separated us, she mashed the buttons on the outside.

The doors reopened and I rolled off.

"You've got to hold the doors!" I insisted. "And look behind you!"

We were an hour-and-a-half late. We were supposed to meet a man in Baggage Claim that would deliver the wheelchair van. He'd hold up a yellow sign with "Quincy" written on it. If we ever found Baggage Claim.

"This isn't it," my mother said, walking past me again, just as I caught up to her. "We have to go down another level."

I turned around, adjusting the speed. She walked down a hall and took a left turn, going faster. I repositioned the dial and followed her around the corner. Suddenly, she came to a halt.

"Aaaaagh!" she screamed, running away. "You're going to hit me with that thing!"

"Well, yeah, if you stop *dead*. Where are you going?"

"Back on the elevator! I just said we have to go down one more level!" She looked around, confused.

"Here," I said, exasperated. "Follow me." I led the way back down the hall until we came to a moving walkway.

"See? That's not it!" she said, triumphant. "This is where we got off."

"Then where the hell is the elevator?"

We turned down another dark hallway with doors marked "Employees Only." We were definitely off the beaten path. That's the trouble with having to take elevators. Airports are designed for the masses taking escalators. Signs clearly lead the way to Baggage Claim from the escalators. Once you move off course to the elevators, you're on your own.

"How do you lose an elevator?" Mom demanded.

She was on the move again, wheeling her suitcase. I followed.

"Here it is!" I yelled.

We looked at the elevator door as we waited. "It's camouflaged," she said.

A big poster was painted over the door the way they put billboards on buses. It was hard to tell it even was a door. A dozen pink shrimp and a few crab claws looked chilled in a bin with the words "Discover The Market" written below. No "Elevator" sign appeared anywhere near it. We'd gone right by it several times. No wonder we were late.

Jim was late too. Very late. Sent from Accessible Vacations, Jim was a 60s throwback. Tall, skinny and unkempt. He wore cut-offs with an old denim shirt and flip flops.

"I smell alcohol on his breath," my mom whispered when Jim stepped away to answer his phone and light a cigarette.

We sat in the airport parking garage after Jim showed my mom how to secure the power chair with the same tie downs they used on my bus.

"That would explain a lot," I said.

He hadn't known the location of any of the controls. I tried to instruct my mom on how to adjust the mirrors with the automatic levers, only I couldn't see much. It was dark in the parking garage and getting darker outside. It'd taken us all day to get here.

My mother continued to mutter, pushing buttons on the dashboard, searching for the headlights.

"You'd think he'd know the car. That *is* the point of meeting us, right?" she asked. I sat there, helpless.

We left Drunk Jim and made endless laps around the garage, trying to find an exit. It was as if I'd asked my mother to drive an 18-wheeler. She made slow turns, taking nervous inhales between her teeth and peering in the rearview mirror. Like any good fish tale, the van would later grow to the size of a bus.

About 20 minutes down the road, toward downtown Seattle, my mother leaned close over the steering wheel straining to see signs in the non-existent light. It had gone from dusk to definitely dark. I, too, leaned against my window, hoping a sign would come into focus before we passed it.

"It's funny that our lights don't illuminate much of the road," she said.

She was right. There was a barely-lit circle of light in front of the car as we traveled down the highway.

"I mean, look how bright it is around other cars."

I looked. Big halos of lights surrounded other vehicles. Maybe it was the slope of the hood? We weren't used to a mini-van.

Just then, a mini-van passed us, lighting up the road. My mom pulled at the dashboard.

"Unless *these* are the lights and not the brights." The area around us lit up.

Jesus Christ.

"Mom! Those *are* the lights!"

"Then what did I have on?"

The parking lights. For the past 20 minutes and God knows how many miles we had been careening down the interstate in near-total darkness, visible only by two tiny squares of yellow light.

"Stupid Drunk Jim," my mother said.

When we pulled into the parking lot of the Marriott, I told my mother to valet it. There was no other option. The hotel charged an additional $36 a night for this forced convenience. When I made the reservation online, it was a sore spot for me. By the time we pulled in, I'd have paid much more.

My mother pulled into the big circular driveway lit with potted palms, and uniformed bellhops immediately surrounded us. I wondered how often they helped travelers in wheelchair vans. Not often, I guessed from the way they hovered around my mother as she fiddled with the keys to the passenger door. I sat alone inside, a prisoner waiting to be sprung.

Ka-chung!

The locks unlatched and the side door slid open. My mom began to step into the van to unfasten my wheelchair. Just then, I remembered the automatic ramp.

"The ra--!" I screamed incoherently. I couldn't form my words quick enough.

The ramp came out just as my mother's foot came down. The result was that she was walking in place, as if on a treadmill, while the platform spooled out. She had a dazed, slightly confused look on her face, not sure what was happening, but knowing enough to keep walking.

The car behind us took this opportunity to pass us on the ramp side. The ramp finished extending its full eight feet, missing the car by mere inches as it passed. Disaster averted. We all, bellhops included, breathed a sigh of relief.

Later that night, dining on muffins and decaf from the Starbucks downstairs, my mom and I eyed the fluffy queen-size beds.

"I'm exhausted," Mom said, collapsing onto the nearest one. "We don't have to get back in that van again tomorrow, do we?"

"No," I said. "We're here two nights. Everything is close."

"*Thank God,*" she said. And then, "This is *not* relaxing at all."

I thought of what was to come, none of which was necessarily relaxing. I sighed, day one complete. Are we having fun yet?

OUT OF THE GAME

"**D**o you mind telling me how old you are?" she asked. She was Andrea Saunders, manager of the Sunns Adaptive Sports and Recreation Program. My mother was concerned about socialization. She thought it important I hang out with other people in wheelchairs. So Dr. Sweeney had suggested I call Andrea.

"I'm 37," I replied.

"Man! Everyone's younger than me!"

I laughed.

"It's a fun bunch. Mostly in their thirties. Some younger, some older."

By the time we hung up, it was decided. For reasons still beyond my comprehension, I would try wheelchair tennis.

I was terrible. In her defense, I'm sure Andrea had never seen ataxia as severe as mine. There was a guy there who'd had ataxia and double vision, and he said they simply went away. I hung my hope on that fact for another year-and-a-half before giving up.

Then again, Andrea was an occupational therapist, and I'd told her on the phone that my right side wasn't very functional. Maybe I should've said not functional. *At all.* How on earth did she expect me to serve, let alone return a shot with my left hand? I wished for about the bajillionth time I was left-handed.

But being good at the sport wasn't really the point. At least it was secondary to the main points: fitness, fun and friendship. That's what the brochure advertised. In other words, socialization. My mother was thrilled.

The group that met that first autumn Monday night was made up of mostly spinal cord injuries. There were a couple of brain injuries, including myself, and a handful of other ailments that were defects from birth, such as cerebral palsy or spina bifida.

I quickly learned the handicapped hierarchy. Paraplegics, people paralyzed from somewhere around the waist down, are the cool kids on the disabled schoolyard.

I couldn't believe all the things they could do. With perfect upper body strength and control, they whipped around the court popping wheelies and joking around. I listened as some of the gang made plans to meet for a beer afterward. They invited me, as the new girl (they were all very nice), but I declined. I imagined myself with a ridiculous straw in my beer and having to repeat my order to the waitress until someone with a normal voice did it for me.

No, I shook my head and smiled at the invitation. What would I do? Have my mommy drop me off? These people had their own cars outfitted with hand controls and drove themselves. I was never as shocked as after that first night of tennis, watching several people get out of their wheelchairs to put them in the trunk and move to the driver's seat. I have to remind myself now that some people in wheelchairs can walk short distances.

For one of the few times in my life, I didn't fit in. Then I realized this is how it must feel to be ugly or obese, and I stopped the pity party. And those people don't get the compassion someone in a wheelchair gets. They just get the repulsion.

My status as most disabled on the tennis court didn't stop me from developing two crushes. It was early on in my recovery, and I still had delusions about my ability to attract members of the opposite sex. Self-esteem of the physical body takes a long time to dissipate. My inner self-esteem, on the other hand, remains very much intact.

The first of my infatuations was with a paraplegic named Greg. Everyone loved Greg. Good-looking, strong (as far as his upper half was concerned) and someone who took charge, he always helped newcomers with a piece of equipment or inspected faulty chairs. The feelings ended as quickly as they began, due in no small part to his massive ego, which being in a wheelchair did little to curb.

My feelings for Kevin were longer lasting. He had kind eyes and uneven dimples. Unlike Greg, he seemed shy and unaware of his good looks. Being disabled your whole life can do that to you. Kevin had spina bifida and walked short distances with crutches that fit around his arms.

It wasn't long before I gave up Kevin and crushes for good. A few nights on the court listening to my new peers flirt and laugh was all it took. I was no longer capable of witty repartee. I realized that voice plays an integral part in personality. It wasn't my wheelchair or lazy eye that had taken away my desirability, although they hadn't helped. It was my voice.

I did form friendships within the group, as the brochure promised, and I moved on to other activities. I went to adaptive rowing or aquatics every week and tried special seasonal events, like hand-cycling and body surfing. My love of horseback riding was rekindled through the program, and I began to learn that many sports had simply changed, not become off-limits.

I met people of every disability imaginable, and my obsession with determining who had it worse ran rampant. I decided the amputees had it the best. With a good prosthetic, you often couldn't tell they were disabled. At the other extreme was the young man whose face had been burned in a chemical explosion. He could walk, but you could barely pick out the parts on his scarred face; the rest was unrecognizable.

Things even began to look worse for the cool kids. Paraplegics have a lot of junk in their lockers. There are bladder issues, and many have leg bags of urine or catheters tucked out of sight. Some have trouble regulating body temperature because they don't sweat below the spinal break. And they're at risk for injury because they don't feel heat or pain. All problems I don't have. Suddenly my garbled speech didn't seem so bad.

The level of injury and whether or not the break is complete mean everything in the spinal cord injury world. Breaks above the first thoracic vertebrae result in quadriplegia, below it, paraplegia. Quadriplegics have varying abilities when it comes to finger, wrist, arm and shoulder muscles. Or they may not be able to move below the neck. People with spinal injuries can rattle off their stats like a social security number. "I'm a T-4 complete para" or "I'm a C-6 incomplete quad."

Earlier that spring, I learned I was a quadriplegic. My mom and I laughed, assuming someone had made a mistake on the medical form we were looking at.

"Actually," Riley told us, "Amy is technically quadriplegic because she doesn't have good use of any of her limbs."

Mom and I were dumbfounded. I'd never considered myself anything because I wasn't paralyzed. And if you asked me, I made darn good use of my left hand. I did everything with it. But now I had a title. Quadriplegic.

I attended Quad Rugby tournaments as a spectator. These quadriplegics were brutal. Often you'd hear the clashing of metal and see players tipped over in their wheelchairs, waiting to be righted by a referee. Guys love contact sports. Even disabled guys. The sport had a nickname -- Murder Ball.

Later on, I found it. The sport in which I was no longer the most disabled player on the team -- Power Soccer. The game appealed to my sense of humor. The objective is to get an over-sized soccer ball into a goal without using any part of your body. It's like bumper cars except you're not supposed to run into each other. You just drive your power chair, outfitted with a custom metal leg cage, up and down an indoor basketball court. I found it fun and funny.

Unfortunately, I was bad at that, too. My older power chair was too slow. I couldn't keep up with the action, and it seemed I was always at the opposite end of the court from everybody else. The best players had the fastest chairs and were adept at handling them. One of the stars of the team was Brent, born without arms or legs. He sped around using a mouth stick to drive his chair. I wasn't any good, but at least I could take the court without becoming the main attraction.

I recently read the autobiography of a quadriplegic. Desperate for guidance, he visited an Indian guru who said, "Listen, my son. You are fortunate. You are in an excellent position for spiritual growth." At the time, he wanted to strangle the guru, but he later came to embrace the message.

I've come to certain beliefs of my own. I may no longer be in the game, but I had a good run. Besides, I don't think I'm here to find a mate. In a way, I am fortunate. And in an excellent position.

AT THE MOVIES

There's no one to blame but myself. I have willingly followed my mother into this predicament. I'm standing, left arm on the hand rail, right arm around her shoulders, climbing the steps of the movie theater, dozens of eyes turn from dancing hot dogs to watch me. My wheelchair is blocking traffic six or seven steps below. I'm sure people are watching my backside too, as they pile up behind the obstacle we've created.

"Grab me," she says. "We can do it."

What makes me believe her? Why, when I know full well we can't? My mother can overestimate us. My abilities and her strength grow in size whenever she's faced with a challenge. In her eyes, we morph into superheroes. It sucks me in.

Then I wake to find myself in mid-air without a cape, crashing down to the pavement. Or in this case, down to the sticky theater floor in front of everybody waiting for the 6:50 showing of *The Bourne Ultimatum*.

Content just to watch a minute ago, people spring into action. I am manhandled like a sack of dirty laundry, hauled off the floor and into a seat by a middle-aged man. My mom heads back down the steps to get my bag and move the wheelchair. I brush off bits of dirt, hair and popcorn, breathless from my exertions to get here.

I know exactly where we went wrong; I could've told you even before I left the wheelchair. And it has everything to do with the three-foot gap between the handrail and the first aisle chair. It doesn't matter how high we went. I could've climbed to the very back row. I could've climbed all day with a hand rail. But once my mother deemed us high enough for optimal viewing, it was time to walk over, not up. To leave the hand rail. A brief argument ensued.

Mom: "Okay, now just head for the chair."

Me: "Sure. Just head for it. Easy for you to say."

Mom: "Well, Amy, don't think about it so much!"

Me: "Oh, right. Don't think! Are you a physical therapist now?"

Mom: "Oh, for crying out loud. Just grab that seat!"

Me: "It's too low -- "

Those were my last words. I hit the floor after that. And then I was being lifted. No "Hi. How are ya?" No "What can I do to help?" I ceased to exist as a person. I was an item on the floor that needed to be picked up. My underarms hurt through the whole movie from where I'd been hoisted.

That episode on the floor wasn't one of our first times at the movies, but it was one of the worst. I like arriving super early to avoid having an audience for the whole finding a seat process. My mom and I often sit in bright, empty theaters while ushers sweep popcorn off the floor from earlier showings. Our own private "First Look."

Of course, I shouldn't care what kind of spectacle we make getting to a seat, because by that point I've probably already been humiliated at the ticket counter.

At our theater, it's a little-known fact that a handicapped person plus one can get in for the price of one. The "assistant" gets in free.

I guess the idea is that the disabled person might have wanted to go by herself and shouldn't have to pay double just because she visits the restroom and needs help. (Me, I avoid all liquid consumption, especially the jumbo $10 sodas.)

This discount is also a little-known fact to every theater employee with the exception of management. I can usually be found cringing as some ticket-seller requests a manager over the sound system, much to the dismay of the people in line behind us. He or she then loudly asks if "the handicapped," i.e. me, get a discount. It's like being at the drugstore when some loudmouthed cashier asks for a price check on your foot fungal cream.

Once we make it past the ticket window, I begin to pour all of my hope and prayers into the size of the theater. If it's a big one, I'm okay. The theaters showing the newly released, action packed, blow 'em up blockbuster with the half-hour car chase scene are best. *The Bourne Ultimatum* had been in one of these big theaters, with the handicapped seats in the middle and steps up or down, last month. We had waited to see it, and I paid the price. If we're interested in some little film festival docu-drama with subtitles, I can forget it. Chances are, it's showing in some back theater. And the farther back we go, the greater the chance the handicapped seats will be in the very front row. And that means climbing.

No sane person wants to watch a movie like you're watching a game of tennis just to follow an on-screen conversation. Having learned my lesson from *Bourne,* I only climb on my feet if I'm with two people. Otherwise, I'll butt up (which I hope is self-explanatory). Another reason to get there early and avoid subjecting fellow patrons to *that.*

One time I climbed with the help of my mother and a friend. My mother brought up the wheelchair since it fit down the aisle and we could get to "prime viewing location" (the exact middle). In an otherwise empty theater, would you believe a couple carrying snacks galore came and sat in the row directly behind us? My mother actually turned around and said. "I'm sorry, but what *exactly* is the thought process here?" No response. They sat there while we moved, carrying out the whole production of my transferring back into the wheelchair. I told my mom they were probably scared to move because they thought she was a serial killer.

If all else fails and I'm stuck in the first row, I'll ask for my money back. Price check on a handicapped refund.

37 AND 10

I can't believe my parents were ever married, much less in love.

My mother has a party to watch the Academy Awards each year since she's often seen most of the films with nominations beforehand. My father last saw *Wild Hogs* and watches WWF wrestling with my step-mother. My mother's sense of humor is a bit dark. We've been known to crack up over trying to situate my butt over a bedpan. My father's jokes are so corny they should all be followed by the *pa-dum-pah!* of a drum and cymbal crash.

At first, the differences must have been intriguing, but they finally called them irreconcilable in 1980.

My father re-married in 1981 to a woman I remember seeing throughout my childhood. As cliche as it is, Debbie was one of his college students when he was an adjunct Ecology professor at Florida International University.

To my mother's credit, I was never certain of my father's infidelity until I was in college and asked her about it. They always made nice for my benefit. On the surface everything was cordial. To my many pals, also in the throes of divorce, I bragged that my parents remained friends.

Not that there wasn't lots of fighting. There was. The day my father left, he said goodbye to me through tears while my mother hollered, "Don't you dare cry. Don't you dare." But he already was. Her shouting just made the whole scene worse.

Now that I'm older, I sympathize with my mother. But back then, she was always the one yelling, and he was always the quiet, pitiable one with the misty eyes. I felt sorry for him.

As much as I know better now, I can't seem to stop the flow from my bleeding heart when it comes to my dad. This annoys my mother to no end. But I plead innocent. Emotions that stem from childhood cannot be swayed by rational thought. Not without a lot of expensive therapy.

Like the way I still refer to the other one as Mommy or Daddy when I'm with each of them. I haven't called either of them that for thirty years, but I guarantee you if I'm talking about him to her or her to him, my language reverts back to when we were all together. And they do it, too. "Is Daddy coming to visit?" my mom will ask. We're stuck in time.

When my father does visit from Hobe Sound, a small town north of West Palm, he leaves the same day. Debbie is with him, of course. She's our buffer. It might be awkward without her.

My father has this way of seeming embarrassed even when he's not. Maybe he's uncomfortable in social situations. Maybe it's a general self-consciousness attached to his size -- he's somewhere in the neighborhood of 6'4", 250 pounds. He's kind of like Chewbacca, intimidating to look at, but really very sweet.

He's super nice to strangers. He goes out of his way to help waiters and waitresses, always scraping everyone's salad plate and stacking them in the center of the table. This sort of apologetic nature doesn't bode well for me. I need people to go out of their way for me and mine, not the reverse.

At my favorite restaurant recently, when I needed to wash my hands, my dad gave me a squirt full of anti-bacterial soap because a large party was spread out in front of the restroom door. I was denied soap and water so my father could be spared any unease, all for the comfort of a group that probably would have been happy to move.

Contrast this to my mother, the activist. She once took me to the bathroom, even when I didn't have to go, to prove a point to restaurant staff that their aisles were too narrow for a wheelchair. She barreled through, dislodging people from their seats to move tables while I turned every shade of red imaginable.

At a wedding I attended, my father pushed the wheelchair in a long line to the reception. People held the door for us, but he refused, insisting there wasn't room beyond the door for a wheel-chair. Meanwhile, at least 20 people looked at us and inched toward the walls to make way for us. My step-uncle chided him. "What do you think you're driving there? A Mac truck?"

My mom, who expected people to hold the door, would have pushed me in regardless of the space, and rolled over someone's foot.

If my mom is the bull in the china shop, my dad is the squir-rel, nervous and skittering about. Neither should be there and shit's going to get broken.

When I'm with my dad, I long for my mother's assertiveness and bold, protective nature. When I'm with my mom, I want my father's extreme courtesy and polite sense of decorum. I may have a "grass is greener" approach to them separately, but I've never wanted them together.

Even as a child, I never wished, like most kids, that my parents would get back together. As an adult, before the hemorrhage, I enjoyed individual relationships with both of them. I used to drive south, to Hobe Sound to visit my father, to Miami, for my mom. I even had the holidays worked out into a routine. Thanksgivings were spent with my father, Christmases with my mom.

But now, since I'm unable to drive and control the visits, everyone converges on me and Mom in Neptune Beach. The first Thanksgiving I was out of the hospital, my mom hosted the big feast. Everyone was there. My mom. My dad. My step-mother. Friends of my mom's from college. Relatives on my dad's side. While everyone oohed and ahhed at the ocean view from my mom's living room window, I wished I could run down there for a quick swim and never come back. The only other person who seemed uncomfortable with all this togetherness was my ninety-year-old grandmother. She kept calling my step-mother by my mom's name and vice versa. When it came time for goodbye hugs, and my parents embraced, she got so flustered you'd have thought they were committing adultery right there on the spot. She didn't like seeing my parents hug anymore than I did.

I've worked hard, but I'll never truly be independent again. I receive Social Security Disability, but it's not enough. My mother says, just like when they split up, that since my dad can't be there physically or emotionally, he will be there financially. He pays my rent now like he paid my college tuition then.

I am 37 years old, going on 10. My parents are fighting over money. The only difference between now and then is that I don't hear it anymore. The clues are subtle. There's no yelling, just pointed questions. "Is that a new Jeep Mommy's driving?" "Daddy didn't leave a check?"

When you're little you think that once you're all grown up, it will be different. You think that once you make your own money, it will be okay. They'll never have to see each other again.

I am 37 and I am 10 and I've done the impossible. I've brought my parents back together.

ETIQUETTE

A friend once asked me for some inside information on etiquette. Her experience had been that her nephew didn't like being called handicapped. I can't say that's true for me. I don't *like* it, but it is what it is. I *am* handicapped. But I can certainly appreciate his wish. I think these things have to be handled on a case-by-case basis. There are no one-size-fits-all rules of etiquette for the handicapped.

Take the word "handicapped." I prefer the word "disabled." I detest the word "crippled." I'm not even sure it's proper. I think it's like saying "retarded." But it's even worse. "Crippled." From the Dark Ages.

I once went church shopping and found myself sitting through a play in which actors with various afflictions were saved by Jesus. The troubled souls had signs around their necks naming their burdens, in case you couldn't figure it out. The alcoholic staggered around taking mock swigs from a bottle. Someone with dark glasses tapped a long stick. My ailment was less obvious. Just a guy in a long robe with a sign that said, "Crippled." I suppose I could've helped them out if my power chair could've made it up to the pulpit.

Toward the end of the skit, a Jesus in Birkenstocks and a fake beard came around and clapped everyone on the forehead. One by one, they took off their signs. They were healed. The alcoholic didn't look about to fall from the stage, and the blind man could see. The crippled guy? Well, he looked the same, but he wasn't wearing his sign, so I knew he wasn't crippled anymore. I left feeling offended, but it took until later that night to sort out the reasons why.

What bothered me most wasn't the use of terminology I hated, nor the idea that miraculous healing could be obtained with a clap on the forehead, but the notion that my predicament was somehow within my control. Accept Jesus, receive salvation. It suggested that God had punished me or that I'd sinned and didn't know God. I *know* God. I have long, personal conversations with Him. And He agrees it's not my fault.

As for churches, I kept shopping. But even this example depends on the person. A handicapped person with a different belief system might have been comforted by the production.

You have to look at the individual. Some people may want to try to do things themselves. It's best to wait for this type of person to ask for help. Not so with me. I love it when folks step in. I have a hard time asking for what I need. My mother will watch me struggle with a button and not offer assistance until I'm ready to cry with frustration. She insists that I learn how to ask for help. I'm reminded of Sandra Bullock's character in the movie *28 Days,* who, in rehab, has to wear the sign around her neck, "Confront me if I don't ask for help." Really, Mom? I'm learning how to be in a wheelchair probably for the rest of my life. Do we really need to tackle this issue, too?

Many people, however, prefer to operate like Miss Manners. They want some concrete rules. To this group, I give the following advice.

Offer to carry things, move chairs from a table or obstacles out of the way. And go out of your way to open doors. Even from several feet away. Don't assume that the closest person will do it. Getting through doors, whether alone or being pushed, feels like approaching an obstacle course for the Navy Seals.

My mother and I have conducted an unofficial study, and we've realized a rather interesting trend during our research. Most of the time, it's a woman, not a man, who opens the door or offers to help in some way. This helpfulness also appears to be generational. We've had older, even elderly, people rush to our aid while younger, healthier individuals stood by and watched.

One time, we neared a door a young couple stood in front of, and the woman nudged her partner to alert him to our presence. He then promptly *got out of the way.* As we began to struggle, a boy who couldn't have been older than eight came from across the room to hold the door for us. We thanked him profusely in loud voices, as much for his benefit as for the clueless adult. A young boy, he'd learned manners against all odds. I can only guess that his grandma raised him.

And while I'm doling out rules, here's an important one. Absolutely no motorboat noises. I'm referring to the little *vroom vroom* race car sounds that many grown adults seem to find irresistible when behind a wheelchair. I guarantee no one in a wheelchair over the age of six ever found this cute or amusing.

My father is a big fan of the motorboat noises, but then he often does something to break my handicapped rules. Like the time we went to a restaurant to celebrate the holidays and my 38th birthday. Me, my mom, my dad, my stepmother, aunt and grandma. My disability has brought the whole "fam damily" together, as my father would say.

Dad pushed the wheelchair and stopped just inside the entrance. We all huddled around the hostess station in the crowded restaurant.

In my wheelchair, I blocked all passage in or out. I noticed this. My mother noticed this. My father didn't notice this.

What my mother said: "Pete, why don't you move out of the way?"

What my father heard: "Pete, move out of the way, *you dumb ass.*"

He wheeled me from our place just beyond the doorway to park me directly in front of an ice machine.

"There. Look at that," he said.

He was kidding. I know he was kidding. It wasn't funny.

Later, he made one of his standard jokes when I teased him about his age. "Watch it daughter, or I'll roll you off the dock." This deviated from his usual "roll you out in traffic," since we were at a waterfront restaurant.

The waitstaff made their obligatory chuckles. The women in my family all chided him. My mother looked ready to strangle him.

"What?" he protested. "You wouldn't want me to treat you any differently than I normally do, would you?" came his customary reply.

I wonder.

His way of relating to me hasn't changed. When I was little, rough-housing took the place of more standard displays of affection. As I grew up, our tenderness took the form of teasing, ribbing and all-in-good-fun jabs. Now that I'm in a wheelchair, the fight doesn't seem fair. I'm an easy mark.

Other times, he's told the hostess we were a party of two-and-a-half. I was the half. It was The Curious Case of Amy Quincy. I'd gone from age 38 to eight in the car ride to dinner.

People have a hard enough time knowing how to act without a family member making inappropriate remarks.

But my father isn't the only one to breech my etiquette. Mom's done it, too.

For example, please try to remember that, though in a wheelchair, your loved one is not a child. My short hair has a tendency to grow into a ducktail at the nape of my neck in a way that my mother finds adorable. Unfortunately, this area is now visible to her like never before. She has a tendency to put her arms on my shoulders and play with this ducktail in a way that makes me feel it's my first day of kindergarten.

And finally, think of the view from down here. There are many reasons I don't hang out in bars anymore, but the main one is that I'm now at butt level. That and I could easily take a cigarette to the face. I've been invited to wine tastings where everyone is standing and not drinking from straws. And I've been taken to cafes with nothing but tall bar tables. Still, it's nice to be included. Just don't park me facing the ice machine.

CARETAKERS WORK AT THE ZOO

My mom relishes the use of a particular word lately -- caretaker. I take exception on several different levels, the first of which is that a care*taker* works at the zoo, while a care*giver* aids an actual human being. Also, to give care implies that the person being helped can do some things for themselves. Taking care of someone, on the other hand, suggests dependence, as in: the babysitter takes care of the children.

I am 38 now. I have not required a babysitter for some time. Well, that's not entirely true. Throughout last year, Mom didn't go out of town overnight unless someone stayed with me. As my grandmother says, *"What if you fall out of bed?!"* If I fall out of bed (and it's only happened once after I'd been drinking), then much the same as anyone, I crawl back into it.

My mother drops the word several times a day. To strangers who ask what she does for a living, she replies that she is a caretaker. To friends on the phone she admits with a sigh that she is hanging in there and never knew caretaking could be so hard.

I think she picked up the term from her friend Brenda, who has a sister, Mary, who had a stroke. Doctors told Mary she could regain full function and learn to walk again; however, battling depression, she simply let Brenda do everything for her, and her muscles atrophied. In a letter, Brenda advised my mom to make sure she took care of herself. *"As a caretaker, you need to remember to take care of YOU. Take a mini-vacation. Relax with a book. You need some time off, Suzie."* Ever the martyr, my mother skipped the vacation and trudged on.

I should clarify here it's not like I need 24-hour care. I shower, I get dressed and I make the bed. I transfer myself on and off the bed, toilet, and couch. I make food using the microwave or toaster oven, assuming things are prepared, packaged, opened or poured in advance. I even do my own laundry. We pay a girl named Tonya to clean both apartments every two weeks.

True, the first year was difficult for us both, but while I've moved on, Mom seems to revel in her role, commanding encore performances. I spent a week after Christmas at my aunt Lynn's while Mom stayed home. She said she needed a break. *A break from what, exactly?*

Adding to my frustration is my mother's flair for the dramatic. She got out of a speeding ticket once by saying that she was hurrying home to her invalid daughter. Invalid. I bristled at the word when Mom relayed the story, but she insisted it's another word for disabled. I say it's another word for bedridden. I looked it up and while disabled is there (along with crippled), I am closer to correct. Invalid: a person, usually in chronic, ill health, sickly. I am *not* sickly.

I think Mom knew the word didn't really fit, but she had to avoid the ticket. It's been a running joke ever since. I call myself her "invalid daughter" whenever possible. "It's too bad your daughter's an invalid, or you might've gotten something for Mother's Day," I tease.

In addition to martyrdom, there's another job hazard to caregiving. I call it "Servant Syndrome." It occurs when the caregiver is asked to do so many, often menial, tasks that he or she begins to feel like a servant. The caregiver often complains about not being appreciated and responds with repeated requests for "pleases" and "thank yous." Or, in my mother's case, a sarcastic, "Yes, ma'am." I'm convinced that this syndrome is the result of the nature of the duties rather than the politeness of the requests, because I have heard the caustic "yes, ma'am" even after giving the prerequisite "please."

We pull out of the doctor's office. I sit and look out the window, stewing mad. My mother has been short with me again, acting annoyed, and I am sick of it. Now, as soon as we hit the parking lot, she's fine. My morning is ruined, but she has pushed the reset button and is just jolly.

"Are you angry?" she asks. Her humming stops short.

"Yes."

"What about?"

"You've been snapping at me all morning!"

Now she's mad, too. "Well, sor-ry," she says, not sounding a bit sorry. "But now you know how it feels. You were ordering me around in front of Susan and Dr. Brown!"

Ohhhh. Now we're getting somewhere.

A classic case of Servant Syndrome. She was crabby with me because I told her what to do. I admit, I may have forgotten a few "pleases" and "thank-yous", but I would argue that when you need as much help as I do, there's a point when good manners become overkill.

The next morning, I wake up, still mulling it over. We head to the grocery store, my usual weekly shopping trip. While she motors over in the Publix scooter, I decide to test my theory. I'll say "please" every single time I need something. Since I often can't do something as simple as get a box of granola bars into my cart without dropping it, I am sure to make my point.

"Thank you," I say when she arrives with the motorized cart.

"Can you please get four apples?" I say inside.

"The whole wheat buns, please."

I am spewing niceties until about aisle four, when my mother stops pushing her cart along behind me. I look back.

"Are you being sarcastic?" she asks.

"No, I'm trying to be more polite."

"Well, don't," she says, rubbing her temples. "It's too early in the morning."

Unfortunately, the pleasure I feel over being right only lasts until aisle seven. There I run smack into a display case with a big crash, and we both dissolve in a fit of giggles. With my eyesight being what it is, along with the short height and white color of the wire bin, it never stood a chance. Rice-A-Roni is all over the floor.

I decide to skip the "please," but she is already picking them up. A caretaker's work is never done.

A NEW NEW YEAR'S

I must have been insane to do it. Maybe my ability to reason had not been fully restored. I still operated under my old personality. It was the end of 2007, and the old me loved going out to ring in the New Year.

"Do I have to make reservations?" I asked the voice that answered at Twisted Sisters.

A long pause. "What?"

I'd learned to rephrase. To always use different words. "Do you need my name for dinner?"

Silence. "I can't understand you."

I sighed, then tried again. I enunciated as best I could, which is to say, not at all. "Do I need reservations?"

Click.

"Arrrrrrggggh!" Asshole. Bella pinned back her ears and glared at me from the couch.

I redialed. On the fourth try, I got it right. I shake more when I'm trying to hurry. It's even worse when I'm mad. Five minutes had elapsed. The same voice answered.

"Yeah, hi. You just hung up on me?"

"We must have gotten disconnected."

Big fat liar.

"Can I please speak to someone else?"

"There's no one else here yet."

Bigger, fatter liar.

"Gee, you seem to understand me now."

"Sorry?"

Sigh. "What I'm asking you is if I need reservations."

"No."

Turns out (big surprise) I did. But by then, it didn't matter. My mom decided she didn't want to eat and just dropped me off when we found Vivian in the parking lot of Twisted Sister's Restaurant and Bar.

My mom gave Viv a big hug. "Thanks for bringing her home. You're great to do this. You girls have fun!"

What am I, five? And why does my mom always have to act like my friends were so wonderful just for hanging out with me?

Viv looked cute in tight metallic pants with a black silk scoop-neck and the strappy heels with the high cork wedge I'd passed on to her. I loved those shoes. Even as painful as they'd been after a night out, I loved them.

We waited in a short line. The girls wore tops covered by leather jackets that would later be shed to reveal sparkly colors and glitter and too much skin. I was conscious of my jeans and frumpy black sweater. I wore flat, black boots that might as well have been corrective shoes surrounded by all those tottering heels. These women clacked. I clomped.

The bouncer waved us in without asking for ID. We were old enough to never get carded and young enough to still get disappointed about it.

Viv pushed the wheelchair toward a large empty table up front that had a homemade sign with the words, "Reserved -- Band" on it. Rob came over from practicing to thank us for coming out. He didn't know we were grateful just to have a place to go. I used to love that when we were dating. Viv's husband was in a band too, so we always had a choice of venues.

I get the whole groupie thing. I liked to dance. I liked being on my own in the place or on the dance floor, yet having a reason to be there. I liked having the best table in the house reserved, and a cocktail waitress to check if my free drink needed refilling, while everyone else clamored around the bar. And let's face it. Girls are hot for musicians. It's a law of the universe. Like gravity.

Rob had several things going for him. He was a drummer, yes, but he was also a writer -- a good writer. I fell in love with the drummer and the writer. Both were illusions, of course, smokescreens. When the smoke cleared, I was left with simply a human. And the human fell far short.

There was something else that had attracted me. Rob was tall. A bit nerdy, but a good-looking nerd, like Adrien Brody or Edward Norton. He was 6'2". At almost 5'9", I cared about height. Then. Now, everyone's taller than me.

People parted as we cut across the dance floor on our way to the table. I received lots of attention, "Happy New Year!" wishes and condescending "you go, girl!" pats. Apparently, my very existence among the scene was to be commended.

When we reached the table, I had a moment's panic. It was a bar table. It wasn't so high that I could've rolled under it, so I insisted it was fine. And it was fine if I sat back from it a bit. Good thing I'm tall. When the waitress came over, I ordered my new signature drink. Cranberry and vodka.

I drank cranberry and vodka because it came with a straw. I had done enough time looking stupid with straws in wine glasses. At home, I felt free enough to sip my screw cap Chardonnay out of a big water bottle, but in public I tried to class it up a bit.

I'm not sure why I bothered trying to blend in at half everyone's height with two very large wheels attached, but I did. I don't like to call attention to myself. Hey, the hemorrhage left all my character defects intact. I still have my vanity.

My drink arrived with a coffee stirrer, so Viv had to go up to the bar anyway. I sat cloaked in the darkness of the wall that was next to us, listening to the music. By my second drink, I was drunk. I knew this because I was having to repeat myself more than usual. I slur worse after a few cocktails.

The band played an old Train song. Viv and I had always danced to it. It didn't matter if we were at opposite ends of the bar or if one of us was in line in the ladies' room when it started. We would hear it and run, meeting out on the dance floor.

"Do you mind?" she asked.

"Of course not. Go," I said.

And just like that, she was out on the floor.

I have no rhythm now. I can't chair dance. I can't bob my head. I can't even tap my foot in time. I'm like that cowboy friend of Kevin Bacon's in *Footloose*. The only thing I can do without looking like a total spaz is shake my shoulder. Kind of a shimmy.

I ordered another cranberry and vodka. The song ended. Viv came back, and the band took a break. Rob came over and sat down. He gave me a long look.

"You're drunk," he said. I hadn't said a thing.

In the hospital, he'd been the only one who could figure out what I was saying. Back when all I could do was grunt and gesture. When even my parents shrugged. Well, we had just lived together for three years. I hadn't lived with either of my parents for eons.

"You know me so well," I said.

"What?"

"You know me so well," I shouted, giving new meaning to the word slur.

Hours passed. The band kept playing. Friends I knew through Rob or Vivian came over to say hello. I usually didn't like running into people that hadn't seen the new me -- old co-workers, acquaintances, men I had dated casually. The pity looks, the uncomfortable silence as they tried to figure out what to say. I always wanted to start, "So! You can see what I've been up to. What's new with you?"

This was different. These were good friends of good friends. They seemed genuinely happy to see me.

There were only minutes left in 2007. I thought about where I was this time last year. Asleep in a hospital bed. Natanya was supposed to wake me up. She said she forgot but after I thought about it -- maybe she wasn't allowed.

Viv brought me a plastic champagne glass with a straw bobbing in it. It looked ready to fall out.

I could so easily have not been there. I looked at all the people on the dance floor, Rob behind the drums, the band counting down. Viv put a silly party hat on my head and jumped up and down with a horn in her mouth.

So I wear clunky shoes, drink out of straws and can only shimmy a shoulder. This whole crazy New Year's might be taking place without me. But I was here to see it, to be part of it. I slurped my champagne through a straw at midnight and felt grateful. You go, girl, indeed.

Part III: Independence

MY VALENTINE

Sometime before Christmas, I noticed the "For Rent" sign in front of the one-story duplex down the street. I didn't let myself think too much about it, but when it was still there after New Year's, I called the number. I didn't involve Mom until I made up my mind, and I needed her to sign the lease.

She was skeptical at first, but then had to admit, it was perfect. It was just two houses down. Close enough, yet far enough away. Most of my family worried. I was ecstatic.

Finally, I could get up early or come home late without waking her. I could organize the fridge however I wanted without her mystery, moldy Tupperware containers lurking. And I could shop and hide presents without the danger of her finding them. Which, with the upcoming holiday, was important.

Walgreens was its own corny planet this time of year, oozing sentimentality all over the place. I combed the aisles in my power chair, looking for the less mushy cards, wondering how the employees stood it. It started right after New Year's. Red and pink banners swirled from the ceiling. Rows of cellophane hearts from miniature to jumbo lined the shelves. A stuffed lion held out a cushy pillow that read, *I'm wild about you.* I rolled my eyes at all the commercial fanfare and steadfastly refused to go out to dinner that one night a year, but I used to have high hopes.

When I worked, I sat at my desk like every other woman there and pretended it was a day like any other. You could feel us holding our collective breath when the bells tinkled announcing an entry and hear it released in disappointment when the spring water guy filled up the water cooler.

Some lucky women already had their declarations of love on display in their cubicles. I viewed these bouquets like diamonds on a ring finger. They were affirmations. *Someone finds me lovable. I have been chosen.*

Many years, not dating anyone, I contemplated sending flowers to myself just to avoid the empty desk.

Though not dating someone was preferable to dating He Who Does Nothing. I never understood this. It's so simple. It requires virtually no thought. And I never, not once, met a woman who didn't like flowers. Still, it happens. I know because I have dated several Mr. Do Nothings.

One claimed he forgot, which we all know is impossible if you live in the United States of America and didn't just wake up from a long coma. Another said he was taking a stand against profit-making corporate giants and didn't need a holiday to tell him when to express his love. Unfortunately, he didn't express it any of the other 364 days of the year, either.

I broke up with another man on Valentine's Day itself after eight months of dating and receiving nothing from him but a card with a fart joke on it. I didn't think they even made valentines with fart jokes, but apparently no holiday is too classy. I'm sure even one of the three wise men is letting one rip on a Christmas card somewhere.

I thought my years of angst over the holiday were through when Rob and I started living together. I hid valentines for him to find throughout the day. I snuck one out to his car and stuck it under the windshield wiper. Another gift waited for him to open his briefcase. A satchel full of silver tokens. Good for one massage, good for one kiss, they promised. His favorite candy bar lay in his sock drawer. His favorite beer chilled in the fridge with a red bow on it waiting for him to get home from work. The card I got that morning was all I received. The door chimes at work never tinkled open for me. By six o'clock that evening, we both felt stupid. Him, for not doing enough. Me, for doing too much.

"I'm sorry," I said, unable to hide my sadness. "Holidays were kind of a big deal in my house."

Yet, here I was again at Walgreens with multiple cards in my basket. There were two from me and one from Bella. I also had two chocolate roses, Hershey Kisses in pink and red foil and a Snoopy Pez dispenser. I couldn't resist. But the jewel of all my finds was the Smitten Kitten. When you pressed his paw, he announced, "I love you! I love you!" I tossed him in the pile.

On the fourteenth of February, the knock at the door came early. I could barely see who it was for all the gifts piled high.

"Happy Valentine's Day, Mom."

We exchanged goodies. There was a card from Carlito, my mom's cat. On it, a cartoon cat molded the clumping litter in his box into the shape of a heart. I also received a tacky stuffed bumblebee that sang *Be My Baby* by The Ronettes when you squeezed it. I loved it. Almost as much as my mom loved the Smitten Kitten. I still get phone calls when I hear nothing but silence. And then the recorded voice, "I love you! I love you!"

I happily munched on chocolate and thought how good it felt to finally have a Valentine who loved giving and receiving as much as I did.

"Oh! I almost forgot." My mom raced out to the car. She returned with a pot full of a dozen pink tulips. "I couldn't resist."

BONBONS

What exactly are bonbons? I confess I didn't know. I should have since everyone thinks I sit around and eat them all day. When I found out they're often chocolate covered, with various cream-filled centers, and similar to truffles, I thought some research might be in order. Then I thought better of it. I'm trying to eat healthily. Being in a wheelchair and unable to get any real cardio, I put on weight just looking at chocolate. And working out is one of the things I do all day with my free bonbon-eating time.

My most recent workout routine at home is an hour-and-a-half long. I have a big, blue mat about six feet long and an inch thick. I fall out of my wheelchair onto the mat and do yoga (floor poses) and sit ups. I also have a wall-mounted contraption with a bunch of eye hooks I clip resistance bands to, working out my arms. This exercise is in addition to what I do at the YMCA's pool on occasion, and with Kris on her lunch hour. When I finish with my mat workout, I scoot on my butt the short distance to the living room, rolling my wheelchair in front of me, to pull myself up into a big chair. The living room chair, since it backs up to the wall, is sturdier and easier to get into from the floor than my wheelchair. Factor in the time it takes struggling to get the mat in and out of the closet, add crawl time, and the whole process takes close to two-and-a-half hours.

When calculating time for a disabled person, a safe formula is to double the duration needed by the average able-bodied person to do any given thing. Triple it if getting clean, changed or otherwise presentable. If Carl Capable gets ready in fifteen minutes, it will take me forty-five. Exponentially, if he needs an hour, better give me three. This formula varies according to handicap. My friends have learned not to invite me to any last minute affairs. There's no "pick ya up in a half hour" anymore. I've lost the ability to be spontaneous.

My definition of "presentable" has also changed. A shower becomes far less important when there's an hour-and-a-half of work involved. I have to set up the shower bench, stand up at a pole to undress my lower half, transfer, finish undressing, set up the wheelchair with my shoes and towel and tuck the shower curtain around the bench where it extends beyond the tub. All this before I've turned on the water. When I'm finished, I dry off, put on my shoes and transfer back to the towel-covered wheelchair, hoping I don't slip and break my neck on all the water that's escaped the shower curtain and now needs to be cleaned up. If it's a hair-washing day, add another half hour.

While I've been known to miss a shower or two, particularly on Sundays, I never skimp when it comes to a clean house. I haven't been diagnosed, and it's certainly not serious, but I'm a tad obsessive-compulsive. My books are arranged by both size and subject matter, and I'm a firm believer in "a place for everything and everything in its place." I line up all the frozen foods in my freezer so the labels read left to right, top to bottom. Even my junk drawer is organized.

This behavior, while borderline OCD, is extremely beneficial to my handicap. Since I have to ask other people to do a lot of things for me, it helps to know exactly where the tape/screwdriver/flashlight is. People say I have perseverance, but I know better. I don't spend a half hour closing buttons because I'm strong or determined. I have to wear that shirt or my whole outfit is wrong. I don't continually fight with a zipper because I want the jacket closed. I just can't let it go.

Where this patience doesn't do me any good is on the issue of time. I spent an hour making my bed the other day (of course, I make my bed every day) because I had kicked off and untucked all the covers in my sleep. Imagine me untangling a sheet with one hand, rolling back and forth and back and forth to make sure each side is even, and you begin to understand how my time evaporates.

Of course, Tonya comes twice a month to do all the things I can't, like dust, vacuum, mop and clean the toilet, but I still get up at 4:30 a.m. I tidy myself and the apartment, eat breakfast and write. Then, by the time I return a few emails at the snail's pace of nine words a minute, it's time for lunch. Workout, go to an afternoon appointment or on an errand, and it's time for dinner. I've put quite a few miles on my power chair, and I take myself to any place within a mile radius. This includes the dry cleaner, jeweler, chiropractor, drugstore, ATM, and various restaurants, shops and friends' houses. Add bathroom breaks of ten minutes apiece, and it's a wonder I have time left at all. Before I had a way to stand up in the bathroom, I used to have to transfer to the bed, take off my pants, transfer to the chair, wheel into the bathroom and lunge onto the toilet. Then, I had to do the whole thing in reverse. My friend, Lora, commended me for wearing pants at all. She said she'd have just gone around in a sheet.

I "quit" around 4:00 or 5:00 p.m. In order to be up so early, I'm asleep by 8:30 p.m. It takes me an hour to get ready for bed, plus I like to read first, so I head that way when the sun sets.

One evening, Michele called to see if she could drop off some leftovers. "I was just going to bed," I said.

"It's seven o'clock."

Many people don't understand. They think that because I don't go to work, I'm living the lifestyle of ladies who lunch. Delivery and service people make this assumption all the time. People think they're free to show up three hours later than scheduled or just stop by because I'm in a wheelchair -- of course I'll be home. When it turns out I'm busy, I get teased about my "full social calendar." I guarantee you, I'm booked far less than any able-bodied person who's not a shut-in. Yet I'm treated to sarcasm if I have to tell someone I already have plans. I'm not supposed to have plans.

When I was employed nine-to-five, I daydreamed about calling in sick. I fantasized about what I would do with an uninterrupted expanse of time. These musings always involved large quantities of food (bonbons, if I'd known about them) and daytime television. I could imagine nothing sweeter than watching *Let's Make A Deal* in my pajamas. Of course, now that I can do just that if I choose, it's lost its appeal. The television doesn't come on before *Oprah,* and I still long for that uninterrupted expanse of time.

I don't expect people to understand. Particularly those who work full-time. I didn't get it when I worked full-time.

I asked Michele last month if she'd take me to Walgreens. It's an hour in travel time alone. I said I didn't feel like driving the power chair.

"Why not?" she asked. "What else have you got to do all day?"

YOU CAN'T HANDLE THE TRUTH

"Oh my God!" someone shrieked. Lucy and I turned down a sidewalk looking for an open table. We were at Art Walk together. The third Thursday of every month, all the shops about a mile from my street stay open late, and local artists set up booths outside to sell their wares. We headed to Shelby's, the local coffee shop, for some decaf and a piece of Shelby's homemade fudge. We were still laughing about my near collision with a bush when I heard the scream.

"What happened to you?!" Cindy, a former coworker I hadn't seen for years, looked at me aghast. My laughter trailed off. Christ. There was no escaping her. I turned off the power chair. Lucy stopped next to me. "Were you in an accident?" She looked horrified.

"I had a brain hemorrhage," I replied.

Tears welled up in her eyes. "I can't believe it. I just can't believe it." Her hand still covered her mouth, and she shook her head. "Why do bad things happen to good people?"

"The million dollar question," I mumbled, with a bit more sarcasm than I intended. I'd been going for light-hearted. Here I was, having fun with a friend... I can almost forget until someone looked at me like that. I had ruined her night, and she was well on her way to ruining mine.

"Cindy, Lucy. Lucy, Cindy." I introduced them in an attempt to steer the conversation toward some sort of normalcy. But she held on.

"When?"

After she'd asked her many questions, we moved on. Granted, I'd had over a year to adjust compared to her minutes. But still. Is this the emotional reaction that runs through everyone, only others have the sense to cover it up? She's a prime example of why I don't like to run into people I knew before. Geez. *I* ended up consoling *her*.

While her reaction may have been over the top, at least it was real. A couple weeks later, I helped a new friend Jen, whom I met through Lucy, pick out paint samples at Home Depot. We saw a guy we both knew. He recognized her first. "Hey, Jen." They made small talk and I noticed him stealing sideways glances at me. I cringed. And waited for the inevitable.

"Hey, Amy!" he said, like he had just bumped into me yesterday. Like I was still the cute girl he had forever tried to date. Like I hadn't mysteriously morphed into this new crippled version. "How are ya?"

"Fine," I said, dumbfounded. No questions. No acknowledgement. Just absolute and utter denial. Okay. So this was how we were going to play it. There's a gigantic, polka-dotted elephant in aisle two of the Home Depot, but okay. It never happened.

I don't mean to generalize here, but what the hell? Men are cowards. The only decent, normal reaction I've ever gotten from a man has been when his wife was there to lead by example. Left to their own devices, they choose avoidance. Take these examples:

The man I'd just started dating when all of this happened sent flowers to the hospital. I even received two plush cats from him. Once home, and a good six months since I'd seen or talked to him, I emailed to joke that he was free to date other people and thank him for the gifts. I said little about my disabilities. He sent a prompt reply that he was glad I wrote and had tried to contact me, but my number had changed. He then asked when doctors said I'd be walking again. Here was a man who had no clue what he was dealing with. My next email to him was more enlightening and spelled out my various handicaps. I never heard from him again.

Another former lover sent a goodbye email stating it was too painful to see me this way. He said he'd always be my friend, but it was just too hard. This seemed to be a contradiction. After all, what does the word "friend" mean to you? Gee, I'm really sorry my becoming handicapped is so difficult. For you.

And it isn't just romantic partners that employ the avoidance technique. Men from platonic relationships use it, too. Take the friend I'd known since high school and had seen off and on until about 10 years ago. He found me again on that demolition social site called Facebook, where I lived in fear of wrecking balls from my past. It's obvious from my profile picture that I'm in a wheelchair. In fact, if you spend any time at all getting to know my virtual self, my handicaps become pretty clear. Nevertheless, I can only assume he had no idea, because he wanted to "talk" and catch up. When I responded that we'd do better in writing, that he might not understand my speech, he vanished.

Even Riley, who'd been such a rock in those early months, turned into a mere pebble. As a massage therapist who worked for Sunns alongside physical therapists, he told Rob that our friendship had become too much like work. He, too, disappeared. If asked, I'd have chosen the friend, not the therapist. I wasn't asked.

My friend in Colorado, Tracy, laughed as I relayed the meetings with Ms. Stricken and Mr. Blasé.

"So what do you want? What should people say?"

"I don't know. There has to be something between the two extremes," I said.

A month later, I was at Target when an old boss, Diane, approached me. "Amy. What happened?"

I told her.

"I'm sorry," she said. We spent some time talking about old co-workers, some who'd left, others promoted. Then she said if I ever needed anything, a ride or just to talk, to give her a call. I knew I wouldn't call, but it was nice just the same. I didn't even mind running into her. It was perfect. No tears. No shrieks. No polka-dotted elephants.

RISKY BUSINESS

Chances are, I will die in a bathroom. It's the least desirable place to be found, but the most likely scenario. I imagine my last view of this world will be the mildewed, hair-clogged tub drain. No one wants to meet a tragic end naked in the shower or sprawled across the floor with their pants down around their ankles. But it's where I face the most hazards.

Several well-meaning, older relatives have suggested I get the I've-fallen-and-I-can't get-up pendant, but I refuse. I'm only 38. It's not like I'm going to fall and break a hip. Maybe I can't get up, but I will crawl, bleeding from the head if I have to, before wearing one of those things. My cell phone is always with me. Some people argue, "But what if you can't reach it?" To which I say, "And what if I'm knocked unconscious?" No button around my neck will save me then. My point is, when it's your time, it's your time.

And with my shaky incoordination, I'd probably set the thing off accidentally. I don't know if it works like a security system, but if it does, it's fair to say I couldn't afford the false alarm charges.

I've gotten better at negotiating bathrooms over the past year. When I was just out of the hospital, my mother helped me. It's laughable really, how they released us out into the world, out into the wild. I had to stand, steady myself by her shoulders, hoping I didn't fall and take her out with me while she unfastened and took down whatever I wore. Then, I kind of crash landed onto the toilet behind me. We practiced these moves with my physical therapist a few days before I left for home. I'm sure the therapist discouraged me from crash landing, but in reality, that's what happened.

I was too out of it to wonder how I was supposed to accomplish this on my own or if I'd have to be accompanied to the bathroom for the rest of my life. As for her part, my mother operated under the "one day at a time" principle.

When my head cleared, I wanted my privacy back. An internet search revealed all kinds of neat products and mobility aids. Who knew? I could fill a phone book in China with all the things hospital staff didn't teach me. Their concern was in releasing me into some-one's care. My concern was in learning to care for myself.

I looked through lots of catalogs and dreamed about how I'd set myself up. I dog-eared page after page. It was like being little when my grandparents let me pick out my Christmas presents from the Sears and Roebuck catalog. It was just as fun planning what to get as getting it.

Some products make life a whole lot easier. Like the cup with the built in straw for a handle that I rinse my mouth with, the laces that corkscrew tight instead of tying, or the stainless steel, 2-in-1, hybrid silverware -- the sporks (spoon and fork) and the knorks (knife and fork).

Other items, I tried and discarded. Like the "rocker knife" shaped in a half-circle, that you worked in one hand by rocking back and forth. It still required accuracy, a skill I sorely lack. There was also the microwave-safe sippy cup with the hole so big I sloshed liq-uid out of it, and the giant grabbers, a pair of over-sized tongs used for retrieving fallen items. I soon realized that I often dropped food. And that I'd have a mess on my hands if I used big, plastic pinchers to pick it up. It was easier to bend down and use my left hand.

Since I rented, I realized my bathroom independence would not be facilitated by the pricey handicap bars that needed to be drilled into multiple tiles. I opted for a single, inexpensive floor to ceiling pole that allowed me to access both the toilet and the shower, with the pole positioned between the two.

My friend Dana (pronounced like banana) inspected the bathroom on a visit last summer. "Can we talk about why you have a stripper pole in the bathroom?" she asked, cocking an eyebrow.

"Same reason I have a tip jar in the bedroom," I quipped, referring to the jar of change I keep for the bus. It's also why I wear vests instead of jackets, mittens instead of gloves and keep my towels in a rolling bin instead of folded in the linen closet. Simplicity is the key to living the disabled life.

I do fine now in any handicapped restroom, assuming it meets current code. And that's a huge assumption.

Since my anniversary trip to Seattle, I've decided handicapped hotel rooms are the way to go. Let me rephrase that. Nice, new handicapped hotel rooms are the way to go. I've been in older renovated rooms. Big mistake. I've seen one "handicapped bathroom" from the doorway. It wasn't wide enough to actually get into. I stayed in another hotel where I could get in the bathroom but not close the door. This wouldn't have been a problem except that the grab bar was nowhere near the toilet and behind the door. Then there was the time I stood up, and the bar came out of the wall. I sat down in my wheelchair with the bar and pieces of drywall in my lap.

Lucky for me, those stays were only for a night. I took spit-baths and found handicapped restrooms in restaurants. I've since developed a theory about restaurant lavatories: the quality of a handicapped restroom is directly proportional to how mainstream a restaurant is. If the meal can be ordered by a number, as in value meal number two, or comes with a prize of any kind, it's probably a great place for me to visit the loo. A mom and pop kind of place with great food and local art on the wall? Not so much.

My mom and I usually prefer a unique dining experience to chains or fast food. Which is why many an unsuspecting stranger has opened the main door to the ladies room to find my mom and my wheelchair blocking the door to the handicapped stall (the wheelchair didn't fit) and me, just beyond, popping a squat for all the world to see.

Take these restaurant and hotel experiences, and you soon realize it's just easier not to go. I try to limit my consumption of liquids whenever I'm out. In fact, I'm willing to bet that any disabled person you see out in public is dangerously close to dehydration.

The communal outing is still preferable to the average residential guest bathroom. With all its pretty rugs, soaps and perfume bottles, or any of the million other things that can get in the way or be knocked over, it's completely inhospitable to the disabled visitor. The last time I succumbed to the lure of a commode inside someone's home, Tracy and I were visiting Dana outside of Boston.

The three of us first met in our early twenties, working for Merrill Lynch in Jacksonville. Tracy and I were fresh out of college, as evidenced by the Mardi Gras beads still dangling from her rear view mirror, a fact Dana and I loved teasing her about. Dana had already been out in the workforce, utilizing her art degree to dress department store windows.

We were all attractive enough, though not in the conventional, cheerleader-type way. We considered ourselves the cool girls of the new hires. Tracy was the short, tomboy and natural blonde. Dana's hair ranged from reddish-blonde to light brown, depending on her mood and the color in the box that month. She was a few years older and more worldly, in the way of an ex-pothead. And while not exactly the girl-next-door, I was at least the-girl-down-the-street. We were girls who would accept most dares, provided they carried with them the potential for fun.

So from skinny-dipping in night-time waves, to stealing on stage for a picture with the band's equipment, and donning deep, Southern drawls to approach some cute guy, we did have fun. We'd been friends for almost twenty years. I still have the photo of Dana behind the drums and Tracy with a guitar strapped around her neck. Our friendship has lasted, but is now long distance. Tracy and her husband live in Colorado. Dana and her husband live in Boston. I remained in Jacksonville.

At a recent reunion, our trio crammed into Dana's hall bathroom. I broke my own rule and partook of several cocktails. Dana's husband Bryan boasted he made a perfect Mojito, and I justified most behavior with the phrase "I'm on vacation." As usual, I didn't see the decision to drink alcohol through to its end. As a result, I was forced to resort back to toilet transfers that never really worked in the first place, and do so with a full bladder. My balance and coordination had gone from poor to non-existent.

"On three," Dana said. I sat poised with my hands on her shoulders. Tracy was nearby on pant patrol. "One. Two. Three!"

Tracy lunged at the waistband of my pants where I sat. "C'mon! Let's go!" she shouted.

"What the hell?" Dana said. I was already laughing.

"You said on three," Tracy said.

"Yeah, one, two, three, stand."

"That's not *on* three," Tracy said.

"Oh, for crying out loud," said Dana.

"Quit making me laugh. I have to pee!" I said.

A knock at the door. "Is everything okay in there?" Bryan asked.

"Yes," we chimed in unison.

I flew back the next day. Dana drove us to the airport and I said goodbye to Tracy at my gate. I turned down a soda on the flight to Jacksonville. The bathroom on the plane was simply out of the question. I arrived home ready to burst.

Home sweet stripper pole.

POSITIVE THINKING: ENOUGH ALREADY

If one more person tells me to "never give up" or "you can do anything you put your mind to," I'm going to lose it. These inane slogans are often uttered by people who can walk, who never spent a day of their life in a wheelchair. Or if they did, it was after they delivered a baby or had their appendix taken out and were wheeled to the car to hop in.

These cheery catchphrases are only a little more tolerable when they come from someone who spent several months in a wheelchair. A friend of my dad's once told me she knew how frustrating it could be because she had to be in a wheelchair for two months when she broke her foot. Do me a favor, people. Don't try to commiserate.

Worse still are people who've been through some kind of debilitating illness and think that, because of this, we are now comrades. A girl I know showed me her tiny trach scar, as if this made us members of the same exclusive country club. All I could think was, *We are not the same. You're walking around with your regular voice. It's not the same thing.* She also watched me reach for something and told me to "relax and try to focus all my energy on not shaking." *Gee. Why didn't I think of that? Focus. It's a miracle.*

In the hospital, I heard again and again, how all injuries, specifically brain injuries, are not the same. Every stroke is different. I guess a lot of people weren't listening.

My friend Michele and I are on the beach one summer morning, when a woman stops us. I assume she wants, like most people, to ask about the beach wheelchair. But no, she wants to swap war stories. She was in a bad car accident, broke almost every bone in her body, *blah, blah, blah,* and had to learn to walk again.

I'm not a callous person. I have compassion. It must have been a horrible several years, and I, myself, have never had to deal with pain. Chronic pain must be awful. But I don't know this woman. She is a stranger who is walking the beach, and what happened to her doesn't give her the right to my story or the answers to her questions.

"What happened to you?"

I give my pat answer. "I had a brain hemorrhage."

This isn't good enough. "Yes, but can you walk at all?"

"No."

"Why not?"

Why not? Did this woman really just ask me why not?

"It's kind of complicated, but it has to do with the part of my brain that was damaged." I don't feel like explaining ataxia or balance and coordination to her. I don't even know her name.

The sun's shining in my eyes, and I can feel my skin starting to burn. We've been stopped, talking to this woman for a good ten minutes. Michele, in all her sweetness, seems interested in what the woman is saying and doesn't realize she has parked me in full sun. I'm trapped.

The prying woman is talking about herself and how doctors told her she'd never walk again, but here she is. (*Rah-rah.*) And then she says it. "So I'm proof you should never give up."

I can't take it anymore. "I'm sorry to be rude, but we've got to get going. I'm burning." Michele springs into action, and we continue. But not before the woman asks for my email address so she can send me a link to an article she read. It's about some brain research that probably has nothing to do with me.

As I explain to Michele why this bothers me so much, I hear my mother's voice in my head, spouting her AA wisdom. *She had good intentions.* Good intentions. The excuse of every well-meaning fool.

Like a physical therapist I saw who, like many people these days, was in love with eastern philosophy and alternative modalities. Hey, I went to massage school. I do yoga. I've had acupuncture and energy work. I've even listened to Wayne Dyer tapes. But the scientific fact remains that a little nerve in my brain that leads to the cerebellum was damaged.

"Do you want to walk?" this therapist asked me.

No. Walking is overrated. I prefer the wheelchair. "Of course, I want to walk."

He was testing a theory of the powers of the subliminal mind, but I'd never heard a more ridiculous question in my life. This idea that deep down I don't want to walk, therefore I can't, is absurd. The world's on positive thinking overload.

Don't get me wrong. I believe there are forces at work beyond our imagination. The mind is a powerful thing. We haven't even begun to understand or use it. I believe in the power of being positive. I'm one of the most positive people I know. I just prefer my cheerleading with a healthy dose of practicality. I'm positive because I'm a happy person despite my disabilities.

I tried explaining it once to a friend. Just because I roll my eyes at the declaration that I'll be walking one day doesn't mean I'm being negative. What if I were to put all my hopes into one day, and one day never comes? No. I have to be happy today. As I am. In this wheelchair. And you know what? I am.

FUN WITH FRANKIE

By summer's end, my mother decided to get a dog. She named him Franklin, after Franklin D. Roosevelt, but I call him Frankie. Frankie is a Pekingese. Mom fell in love with the breed after we found one lost and wandering. She took that one in and called him Teddy Roosevelt, but his owners came to claim him. His rightful name was unfortunate -- Razzle Dazzle.

Taken as she was by Razzle Dazzle and prone to act on whims, Mom adopted Franklin the puppy. Frankie looks like an all white gremlin. He's fluffy with scraggly ears that stick out. He's equal parts cute and destructive little monster. Mom says she had no idea how much work he would be. I wonder how she could not know. Everyone knows that puppies are like newborns. We're hoping he'll grow out of most of his misbehavior. I long for the day when he realizes it's more common and preferable to defecate on grass than on asphalt. You see, I have been walking Frankie.

It was something I wanted to see if I could do. I can. My mom went with us the first few times to be on hand in case of an emergency and to help me work out the modifications. We quickly realized he needed a harness when he backed out of his regular collar. Luckily, he'll come from anywhere within a two block radius at mention of the word "snack." I carry them with me at all times. They're with my cell phone in a bag on the back of my power chair. My mother is under strict instructions to have her phone powered up and on her person whenever I walk Frankie.

Not that I need her. Some kind stranger often takes one look at the situation and steps in to help. Like at the beach boardwalk, when I had Frankie on too long a leash and he jumped down into the sand. Once that man realized I wasn't just waving to be friendly, he came right over. He could see from down by the water that something was wrong. It's not every day you see a girl in a wheelchair above a dog on the ground with a dangling leash connecting them through the slats. Now I shorten his lead when we stop there. I'm learning.

Most of our problems, however, are poop related. It's important to remember here, that I shake when I try to do anything, only have use of my left hand and no coordination. I am also a conscientious person who believes in picking up after her dog.

One particular day, we traveled only four houses down the road when Frankie stopped to take his customary squat in the middle of the street. I am never pleased to see this. While an able-bodied person might simply pick it up and proceed to the nearest receptacle, I am filled with dread. Picking up after Frankie is a virtual minefield of potential disasters. First, I have to position the chair next to the steaming pile. After I turn the power off, I transfer the leash to the opposite side and wrap it around the right arm of the chair, leaving my left hand free to work.

I practiced the part where I pick it up before I ever ventured out with Frankie. At home, I used Bella's toy mouse. I managed to hold my left hand in the bag, pick up the mouse and use the wrist of my right arm to turn it inside out. Voila.

This practice session failed to take numerous real life situations into account. Like the wind. It blew hard enough on this day to make reversing the bag, all the while keeping my fingers clean, tricky business.

As I concentrated all of my effort on this task, I had the vague feeling that something was going on with my right leg. Since I've lost most of the sensation, I looked down to see what it was. Frankie vigorously humped my leg.

Mortified, I kicked him off. Now, it became a game. I heaved him off and he returned at a run to latch on to my leg again. Over and over this went, the warm bag still in my left hand while I shouted a useless "No."

A leaf blew by, distracting him from our contest, and Frankie took off after it. The unsecured leash trailed behind him after one good tug. I finished getting the bag reversed and fumbled at managing both the bag and the controls. I sped off in his direction.

He caught up with the leaf and was now wholly absorbed in shaking it between his teeth. I advanced from behind him and picked up the leash.

Lessons learned: always secure the leash to my right arm, not the wheelchair, before attending to any droppings. And perhaps most important, ask Mom to take him across the street for a quick pre-walk poop jaunt.

This does not entirely eliminate his need to go to the bathroom. Frankie has many multiple-poop days. I know this because I've been walking him on those occasions. No sooner do I get one mess handled, then there's another.

It's best not to get too cocky after learning all these lessons. Last week, I returned home after giving Frankie his morning walk feeling rather proud of myself. Frankie was learning to stay on my left side and out of the way of the power chair. He had not strained at the leash, nor plopped down in the middle of the road when he was tired. I smiled and greeted neighbors and picked up after him without incident. It was a beautiful day. Birds were singing. Altogether, I thought, it felt *normal*.

I was plugging in the power chair when I caught the first whiff. I checked everywhere -- the wheels, the bag, my hands -- nothing. Convinced I was imagining it, I transferred to the big chair in the living room and put my feet up on the ottoman. And there it was. Encrusted in all the little crevices on my shoe. *Unbelievable. Even when I can't walk, I still manage to get dog shit on my shoe.*

DUIS

My mom finally decided I wasn't an alcoholic about a year after the brain hemorrhage. AA taught her only I could decide that for myself, but I think she was pretty certain. She was around me more then, and got to know my habits. I'm sure this was a great relief to her, but she did seem a little disappointed. She wouldn't wish the disease on anyone, least of all me, but there is some truth to the phrase "misery loves company."

It's human nature to want to meet people out in the world who are like you. Maybe that's why recovering alcoholics become so close over meetings, coffee and shared horror stories. It's why I would like to have a close friend in a wheelchair. And why my mother is famous for surprising unsuspecting heterosexuals with the question, "Are you family?"

I'll let you in on a little secret. "Are you family?" is gay speak for "Are you a homosexual too?" My mother has mortified me on several occasions by asking this of perfect strangers or people she has just met. But I shouldn't be embarrassed, because these people innocently assume she's asking if they are related.

"No, we're just friends," said my new next-door neighbor as he and another guy tossed a football in his driveway. Of course, as my mom pointed out later, he might have understood the question perfectly.

My mom doesn't like to be wrong about this. She likes to claim she can tell but, the truth is -- she has faulty gay-dar. In her eyes, several of my ex-boyfriends were also gay, something I appreciated hearing since it was an easy answer to the puzzling question of why they broke up with me.

One of my exes made her nervous while we were dating. Hell, he made me nervous. That's probably why I liked him. Looking like he stepped off the pages of *GQ*, he had a model's face, surfer's body and a smile that flashed the common sense right out of my head. He did have one thing going for him besides his looks, and that was the way he made me feel -- like I'd had too many hot toddies in front of the fireplace. I didn't care that he smoked, didn't have a car, or tended bar for a living (second sexiest job after musician) -- he was cool. And I was his girl.

What worried my mother was his drinking. He had two DUIs and a suspended license. He also had a restraining order and drunk and disorderly on his record. In short, he was bad. Bad Brad my friends called him. And they were right. He'd never gotten physical with me, but I could see the potential was there. It's what made me run the background check on him in the first place. Trouble was, I kept him around for too long. I liked that warm, hot-toddy feeling. And I was 22.

While I viewed my Bad Brad phase as a temporary fling and wild foray to the dark side, my mother saw it as confirmation that the vicious cycle of alcoholism was repeating itself. I was the Adult Child of an Alcoholic. Of course I would choose abusive alcoholics as part-ners. It was textbook. It upset me she hadn't read beyond the text. At the time, I balked. Didn't she know I was smart? But how would she have known? I was growing up on my own. Spending my young adult years away from her. And, as I said before, I stayed too long.

My head finally overrode my heart after several tumultuous on-again, off-again years. You could hear my mother's sigh of relief all the way from Miami. I didn't give her much cause to worry again till the hospital waiting room.

She must have watched me closely that first year or so. We hadn't lived together since she was drinking and I was dry. Mom's signs I probably wasn't a drunk: 1) I could leave wine in my glass at dinner. This was never intentional. Most likely, I was being rushed. 2) I'm a lightweight. Maybe drinking through a straw does get you drunk faster. And 3) The same bottle of white wine was in my fridge all week. Proof that Michele hadn't been around.

Michele and I became close friends and drinking buddies soon after the garage sale she held to raise money for my beach wheelchair. She hadn't even known me at the time. She's generous and kind-hearted that way. Michele offered to push me down the beach (she lives just two blocks away), then we began having movie nights with wine and big bowls of popcorn that she popped the old-fashioned way, over the stove.

The thing I like best about our friendship is that I don't feel like a charity case. We're just two friends whose personalities appeal to each other. I have a tendency to second guess people's motives. Is someone befriending me for me, or out of some kind of civic duty in which I'm the community service project? I don't know if this happens or not. Maybe I'm paranoid, but I do wonder.

Aside from liking each other, Michele and I agree on a lot -- mainly on what we find funny. When we get going, telling stories and cracking jokes, it can be hard for anyone else to get a word in.

My mom thinks it's exhausting to be around both of us at the same time without her coffee. Then again, Mom can find life exhausting without a continual supply of caffeine.

Michele and I can both be high energy, but she takes it to a whole new level. Running a restaurant, supervising three grown children, and still finding time to bake banana bread for all the neighbors. Not to mention being landlord to multiple rental properties, and selling the handmade jewelry, hair clips and soap dishes she makes from shells she finds on the beach. She can be found most early mornings, scouring the beach in her Tevas and halter tops, sandy blonde hair pulled back in one of her clips, as she picks up any shells with holes, all sea glass and interesting driftwood.

The fact that she's in the service industry, divorced, and without kids living at home is handy for our friendship. We're able to share a morning coffee in her driveway when I walk Frankie, or something stronger in the evening when she has the random weekday off.

She put a ramp to her house so I can make it up the step to her front porch. She comes to my apartment a lot, but it's nice to be able to drive the power chair down the street to her house for a change. Doing so makes me feel independent and free. Getting there is always the easy part. Making it home in the dark after a bottle of wine is more of a challenge.

I have a flashlight and clip-on taillight so I can be seen, but I don't trust my vision, so Michele usually escorts me home. So far, there have been two drunk driving incidents. And one time I ran over her foot, perfectly sober and in broad daylight.

Ever since I drove over her toes, Michele keeps her distance. She walks beside me with a good five feet between us, or she hops on herself to take over the driving. She thinks unimpaired by double vision, that she can drive better than me. Trouble is, most times she's jumped on my lap she's been impaired herself, and let me tell you, being familiar with the chair makes me a better drunk driver.

Although, the one time she let me take the last street by myself, I drove into a flower bed next to the side of the road. I was able to push myself backwards out of the dirt using my legs.

The most recent incident, or shall I say accident, was completely her fault. Coming home one night, she jumped on my lap and took over the joystick. As we turned into my driveway, I knew we were going too fast.

"Slow down!" I hollered. A neighborhood dog started barking.

"We have to make it up the ramp!" she yelled back.

"You're going too fast!" I insisted. "Don't you think I've done this before?" I tried to move her hand off the control.

"Stop! You're going to crash us," she said. By this time, we were speeding up the ramp and heading straight for the brick facade on the front of the house.

"*You're* going to crash us," I yelled, but it was too late.

Michele screamed and stuck out her legs, taking her hand off the control and halting the chair just inches from the wall.

"Son of a bitch!" she yelled, hopping off.

In the end, she fractured one of her little toes. The nail turned blue and fell off. I'd have paid good money to be there every time she had to explain why she was limping. Imagine, "Oh, I was driving a power wheelchair and ran into a brick wall."

Friends really shouldn't let friends drive drunk.

FALLOUT

Today, I am a freak.

An article about me, a very nice article, came out in the Sunday paper. I am an inspiration, people say. I don't want to be an inspiration. I'd just like my eyes to look in the same damn direction. Is that too much to ask?

Apparently, it is.

The very nice and inspirational article told readers to visit a website for a video of me. And there I am. Behold, the freak.

I've never seen myself as others do. In my head, I retain more of who I used to be. But the video camera doesn't lie. My lips move but don't match the garbled words coming out of my mouth. My left eye appears to be looking at the camera while my right eye is looking somewhere else entirely.

Friends email me. "You look good!" Or, "Your speech has improved so much!" And I think *Good Lord. What was I before?*

Old boyfriends who haven't seen me or don't know what happened run through my mind. *Oh God.* No matter who broke up with whom, I can hear them, "Dodged a bullet there."

I have seen myself in the mirror, but only in brief glimpses. Never talking or gesturing. No wonder people think I'm retarded. Excuse me, mentally challenged. I used to say "retarded" before I became disabled and more sensitive. Rob always corrected me. He worked summers in high school at a camp for mentally challenged adults.

I'm pretty sure my eyes have gotten worse since I had surgery to correct the double vision. The surgeon said my eyes might align to see one image over time. That was last summer. I still see double, and they look even more misaligned than before. I've noticed it in photos.

So the Monday after the article came out, my mom and I headed to Gainesville. I had been referred to an expert in strabismus surgery -- surgery to align the eyes. We took Frankie, since the trip would take longer than he could stay in his crate. And then it took even longer than that.

We waited for two hours past my appointment time before giving up. I endured endless tests with prism blocks administered by some assistant to the expert we'd driven to see. My mother alternated between going out to the car to walk and water a panting Frankie, and shifting in her seat next to me blowing out exasperated puffs of air. If I'd been alone, I would have waited. I'm a patient person. My mother is not. Plus, we worried about Frankie and his potential heat stroke.

But I did find out from the junior doctor what I wanted to know. Yes, they could make my eyes straighter, but chances are my double vision would get worse. I don't know why this hadn't occurred to me. My left eye sees the clearer, more steady image. I focus on that version and ignore what the right eye sees. If the surgery makes me look better, the images will be closer together, making the right eye version harder to ignore. I think about my writing. I imagine two keyboards overlapping even more than they already do. It's not worth it.

Later that night, I get an email from Jen asking if she can forward the video link to the Never Quit event coordinators. Never Quit is an organization created to educate the public about brain bleeds and their prevention. They sponsor a 5K beach run every year. Last year, Jen pushed me in the beach wheelchair and I heard we made it on television. The newscaster assumed I was a survivor. No one asked for technicalities, but I didn't survive that kind of stroke. I didn't have high blood pressure or heart disease. My stroke couldn't have been prevented. I was born with the malformation that caused it.

Nevertheless, Jen wants me to go. I feel bad, but I don't want to.

My presence at that kind of event always makes others feel good, reminds them that there is a cause behind the free bananas and t-shirts. But it makes me feel worse -- pushed along in my giant dune buggy wheelchair while everybody runs. I tell Jen no.

The next day, Michele calls. She's excited because the article prompted some woman to call about her son. He was in a bad car accident. He walks with a walker. He's having a hard time dealing with his handicap, and the mom thinks it would really help him to meet someone with my positive attitude. Maybe the four of us can get together.

Let me get this straight. The girl in the *wheelchair* with the slurred speech and the lazy eye who can't drive or write by hand or work is supposed to cheer up some guy who's depressed?

Michele is waiting for an answer. "Isn't that beautiful?"

She doesn't understand. Doesn't know what a bad week I'm having. "You can really help people," she says. "Inspire people."

We've had this talk before. Michele sees me giving motivational talks to large rooms full of handicapped people.

I detest public speaking. I hated it when I could speak clearly.

I agree just to get her off the phone. She's the best friend I've got these days, but sometimes she can sure sound like my mother.

They've been taking rides on the same bandwagon.

"I really think something will come of this, " my mom says, referring to the article. "Your chance to do service."

Service. What Michele and my mom and Jen are doing is trying to make sense of it all. If something good comes out of the bad thing that happened to me, then the world has meaning. But if the bad thing happened to *me,* then don't *I* get to decide what it means?

Well, I've decided. And it doesn't involve being a poster child for adults with disabilities, or showing up at events I don't want to attend. I will do what I've always wanted to do, always done really. Except I'll do it with the increased urgency of someone who's been given another chance. Of someone who knows that we're here for a limited time and things can change at any moment. I'll write.

For me and for others. But mostly for me.

DARK DAYS

My mother thinks I have repressed anger.

"I was wondering when it would catch up with you," she says. I've come to her in her driveway to get Frankie with tears in my eyes, describing the loss of my favorite necklace.

"Huh?" I'm confused. I'd been talking about how the magnetized clasp came loose too easily.

"I don't think all this is really about a necklace."

"It's not?" I ask, sniffling, wiping the snot from my face.

"No. Your reaction is much bigger than a necklace. I think you're angry about what's happened to you. The necklace is just an outlet."

I think about it. I'm pretty sure it's the necklace.

Rob gave it to me for my birthday when we first started dating. But beyond the sentimental value, I loved it. I wore it all the time. It went with everything, and people always complimented it. A local artist had blown the cobalt blue glass pendants. They hung like two teardrops from a silver choker-length chain. I'd owned it for years. Now it was gone.

True, this wouldn't have happened if I hadn't had the hemorrhage. For the sake of independence, I had all my jewelry switched from standard clasps to magnets. I was proud of myself. I rode the power chair to the local jeweler with my necklaces in sandwich bags. Now I put on all my old jewelry by myself, whenever I like.

But the magnets came apart. I looked everywhere. By the bed, in the wheelchair, through the hamper. I called Michele and asked her to check her car and call the nail salon we went to earlier. Nothing. And now my mom tells me I'm overreacting.

I'm famous for overreacting. I always cry. I cry when I'm sad. I cry when I'm stressed. I cry when I'm angry. I love a good cry. I've never been known to repress anything. But Mom thinks this is about my disability because I'm too upset over a necklace. It shows how little she knows the pre-hemorrhage, adult me.

She's gotten to know the post-hemorrhage me pretty well. And until recently, that person was medicated. I was first put on antidepressants in the hospital. Never mind that I wasn't depressed. It was enough that I should be. Or might be in the future. Then again, most of those pills were for anxiety in addition to depression and I *was* anxious. I've always been a worrier, a planner. A control freak even. But never depressed.

My mother recalls a time they tested me on five antidepressants at once. I don't remember that, but then I wouldn't, would I? I do remember refusing to take any pills prescribed by Dr. Wacko. And drilling the nurses about my medications.

While I tried to exert some control on the inside, my mother applied pressure outside. She made copies of all my pharmaceuticals and went up the ladder to the medical director of the hospital.

"If she's on five antidepressants at once, how do you know which one's working?" she asked various white coats. I'm not sure she ever received a satisfactory reply. I do know that the number eventually dwindled to one, Zoloft.

I didn't like the idea of being on something, but twice I tried and failed at weaning myself off the drug. Each time it was out of my system, I had what I can only describe as panic attacks. I would wake up in the middle of the night gasping for air, heart racing, claustrophobic. Much later, I wondered if I had sleep apnea and had stopped breathing.

People always speculate about the bad times. They, like my mom, imagine there must have been some grim and awful realization I went through. A despairing, lonely place I visited when I thought about what I'd become, what I'd lost.

Those nights of panic were the closest I ever came to darkness.

I switched on the light so the blackness couldn't close in on me. Only the glare from my bedside lamp made the walls of my room recede to where they belonged. But in the dark, I could reach out and touch them. During these times, I knew what would relax me. A little fresh air, a glass of water. Maybe something interesting on TV or in the refrigerator. *But I couldn't walk there.* It was like waking from the nightmare only to find out it was true. I was trapped.

So, twice, I returned to Zoloft. There was no shame in staying on the drug indefinitely, people said. Dr. Sweeney's secretary shared that she'd been on it for 17 years. Michele had been on some form of antidepressant for 10. Even my mother knew the benefits firsthand.

"You still feel things, just not as deeply," she said in Dr. Sweeney's waiting room. "Your lows don't become bottomless."

My lows always had bottoms. And besides, I didn't want my highs to have ceilings, either. I wanted to feel great again. I wanted my hope to soar. I hadn't enjoyed a good cry in over a year, and I no longer sniffled at sad movies or happy endings.

I attempted to wean myself off again. Only this time, I eased off even slower. I took four months, at first reducing to just five pills a week. It worked.

The first movie I see in my newly unmedicated state is *Marley and Me.* When Marley dies, I'm a mess. I blubber through the whole last half of the movie, when he's sick and old, his face gray around the muzzle. During the scene of his burial, I sob out loud.

I clap a hand over my mouth, embarrassed that the sound escaped me. Then, I stifle a giggle.

"Shhhhh!" my mother hisses.

I grin through the sticky tears drying on my face. I'm baaaa-ck.

CREEPY CRAWLIES

I have a bug problem. By bug, I mean any of the variety of small creatures with multiple legs that scurry. And by problem, I mean I don't want them in the house, and my lack of coordination makes it impossible to get them out, dead or alive.

I don't like anything crawling on me. Even harmless things like lizards make me scream. I know it's childish, but if it jumps and wriggles its little lizard feet on me, I get the willies. And they're stupid. Even when you're trying to help them. Bella will bring one in to play with or maim. Then, when I try to chase it out with the sliding glass door open wide, it will scamper back inside. Even on the threshold to freedom and the great beyond.

The problem is compounded when Frankie visits. It used to be that lizards only got inside when I left the screen door open and Bella brought them back into her lair. Post Frankie, however, the screen flaps in the breeze, and there's a gaping hole where he ran straight through it. I made the mistake of eating when Frankie was in the back yard. He took one look at me with my bowl and charged. In his defense, I don't think he saw the screen, but even the loud pop as it gave way didn't faze him. He didn't even look back. All creatures, big and small, are now welcome to walk right in when I open my house to a cool breeze.

Lizards can live forever indoors. Just as soon as I've finally forgotten about it and told myself it must have gotten out or died, there it is, sitting on the remote control when I want to change the channel. Now, this is the kind of situation that's no big deal when you can simply get up and move away. When you're in a wheelchair, it becomes as intricate and sensitive as a bomb squad operation. The trick is to move slowly, with no sudden movements -- next to impossible for me at any time, but more so when I have to transfer from my overstuffed chair into my wheelchair. I like to keep my eye on the critter, which is a real safety issue, since I should be watching what I'm doing when traveling midair between seats. Once I succeed in getting in the wheelchair without scaring the lizard into flight, I can secure the premises. This means rounding up Frankie and Bella, both of whom find lizard chasing great sport, and confining them to the bedroom. Then, assuming the lizard's still where I left it, I can begin to plan how to get it out of the house.

The day the lizard was on the remote, I tried to get a tray with my glasses, several remotes, several more books and the lizard outside the sliding glass door. Of course, I was shaking, the tray wobbling the whole way, strewing half the items across the floor until I chucked the tray and whatever was left on it outside. When it was over, I had no idea where the lizard was or if I had killed or wounded it in the shuffle. Then, I saw it outside on the deck and watched with great satisfaction as it scampered away.

My mother came over one time to find a CD rack outside and about 20 CDs scattered about the deck, where they had fallen off their shelves.

"Umm, what happened here?" she asked.

"A lizard was on the CDs. Is it still there?" I had shoved the tall rack out the door the night before. She looked for a moment.

"Yes."

Unbelievable. That lizard spent the entire night outside, perched on my CD tower. I told you they're stupid.

Cockroaches are infinitely worse. They bring out a whole new level of terror in me. I hated them before. Now I'm helpless to get away from them. Besides, in Florida, our roaches are "palmetto bugs." And a palmetto bug is to a plain old cockroach what Freddy Krueger is to Casper the Friendly Ghost.

My mom is one of those people with the natural born ability to handle a bug situation. She can catch a lizard in her cupped hand and relocate it. She can also squash a roach with a shoe and a quick crunch and not run screaming from the room. I think people with this talent should contract their services to us non-bug-handlers. That way, if you don't have someone in the family, or you haven't acquired this benefit through marriage, you can still cope. Marriage was never really part of my plan, but having someone to deal with bugs is a big draw.

Mom has rescued me from many predicaments. One night, when I lived in the unit below her, I went to the bathroom in the middle of the night. There I was, half-asleep on the toilet, when not one, but two palmetto bugs crawled across the tile and, like heat-seeking missiles, came straight for me. I shrieked, jumping back in my wheelchair way too fast. I still have nightmares imagining the horrors of missing the chair. I backed straight out of there, yelling the whole way and careening wildly, scraping the bathroom cabinet and door. My tennis shoe amputated part of one roach and it circled on its back, sending me into a fresh series of screams. My mother burst through the front door and ran down the hall.

"I'm okay! I'm okay!" I shouted. "Roaches," I sputtered, pointing toward the bathroom.

She went in to finish off the wounded one who'd been ditched by his buddy. I sat with tears in my eyes, my naked bottom in the wheelchair, my pajamas and underwear down around my ankles.

"All gone," she reported, turning out the bathroom light.

I loved her then. She wasn't even acting put out. And I woke her with screams that I'm sure stopped her heart.

I know she won't be around forever, and I dread the day I'm left to fend for myself among the bugs. I'm proud of my independence, but when it comes to bugs, I need a plan. Medicare won't see bug saving and/or squashing as medically necessary.

I'm going to have to get married. Or move to Iceland. Do they have bugs in Iceland?

PEE PROBLEMS

I have lost all autonomy. Particularly in an office or appointment setting, often any place requiring a ride. I become a child or worse, non-existent, my mother, all-knowing. She sits with me in the waiting room, filling out my forms. They are ridiculous and lengthy medical questionnaires. *Have you ever experienced any of the following: Anemia?* No. *Hydrocephalus?* I don't even know what that is. *Shortness of breath when walking short distances?* It's complicated.

Mom prefers not to come into the examining room with me, though you can see in the widened eyes of the woman with the clipboard that her presence is desired. Otherwise, the staff is left to deal with me on their own and I have thrown sugar into the motor of a well-running automobile. How will they weigh me? Am I mentally challenged? Can I sit on the table?

We used to go in together until we both got annoyed. Her, at the medical personnel who let her do everything while they watched and waited as if they'd never before handled a wheelchair. Me, at the doctors, always directing their questions at her without even glancing in my direction.

One would think people in the healthcare profession would be more knowledgeable about disabilities. Not so. I find them only a tad more aware than the average citizen and some, not at all.

At one clueless doctor's office about six months into my new status, my mother leaned over to me in the waiting room. "Are you okay going in there alone?"

"Yes," I said. "I was just about to suggest that."

"It'll be good for him," she said, nodding her head toward the doctor we'd seen walking by.

"Earn that exorbitant salary," I said.

Recently, my mother dropped me off outside one medical center. Her red Jeep pulled away soon after she deposited me into my wheelchair. As much as I hate to agree with her, it's good for me to go in by myself. I like to figure things out, and attaining something as simple as a routine physical on my own feels like I just ran a marathon. Besides, Mom knows that when I'm alone, strangers come running to assist. When she's with me, she has to do it all herself.

The day she waved goodbye to me from the circular driveway, I made it up the elevator, through all the doors, to the waiting room where I sat with an enormous sense of pride and accomplishment. I whispered in my hoarse way that I couldn't write, and the cheery woman behind the tall counter signed me in.

When they called my name, I was led to a restroom to produce a urine sample. Any good feeling I'd acquired evaporated. The nurse shut the door behind me, and I was left alone in a pristine lavatory. Across from the toilet, on a little trunk covered with doilies, were plastic cups in tidy rows, snap-on lids in a pile, and a basket of peel and stick labels with a black felt marker for identifying specimens. There was also the metal slot for delivering your fluid-filled cup to a nurse's desk on the other side. I took one look at all that urine gathering equipment and left.

I returned to the front desk and managed a cracky whisper. "I'm not going to be able to handle that stuff," I said.

"That's okay," she said with a smile, at normal volume. "Just leave your specimen on the trunk and I'll come label it."

She didn't understand. I'd be lucky to keep from spilling pee all over the furniture, let alone get any in the cup.

People often underestimate the nature of my handicaps. They look at me and figure the wheelchair is the extent of it when really, that's the least of it. You have to see me in action to fully understand just how uncoordinated I am.

I smiled, said nothing, and faced the bathroom again. Once inside, I grabbed a cup and placed it next to the base of the toilet, running through the motions in my head. This operation required serious planning. Once sitting, I managed to fill a cup about an inch full, peeing in fits and starts, worried about both my aim and the level of liquid. Getting it too high would mean sloshing it. Too low and they might not have enough to work with, making this whole exhausting process for nothing. Once finished, I scrubbed both arms up to my elbows as if preparing for surgery and came out. I whispered to the nurse that my sample was ready and could only hope she got in there before any other patients found my uncapped cup of pee sitting on the pretty, doily-ed trunk.

Managing a urinalysis on my own is nothing compared to the paper gowns. Those things are a flimsy mystery for anyone, but for me, with my poor eyesight, use of only one hand and ataxia, I'm usually still half-naked after the allotted 30 seconds of changing time. I've had one doctor walk in on me, though I'm sure you could hear the rustling of paper and ripping sounds far down the hall.

One place my mother always has to accompany me is the vet's office. Much to our surprise, Frankie is the easier animal. Bella, upset and hulking, massive in her too-small carrier, poses much more of a challenge. If we're lucky, a technician will see us coming or already be in the parking lot assisting someone else. Then my mom can get me in the wheelchair while the vet tech handles Bella. My mom was foolish enough to schedule back-to-back appointments for both animals only once. She struggled in, pushing me in the wheelchair with the cat carrier balanced across its arms and Frankie tugging at the leash. She's like that bringing in groceries, too, desperate to get it all in one trip, yet leaving a wake of fallen yogurt and squished bread in the driveway.

We've spent a lot of time at the vet's office lately. Bella had kidney stones. Whenever something arises like this, some kind of subject about which we both know nothing (like kidney stones, carburetors or money markets) my mother becomes an expert. *If* a third person is around. With me, she's free to be baffled by printers and cell phones alike, but with a third party present, she knows it all.

In the vet's office, with the stench of urine and disinfectant in the air and muffled barking coming through the walls, my mom and I wait for the results of Bella's x-ray. I lean over the metal table, petting her as she stretches and lounges, recovered from the drive over and happy to be out of the cramped carrier.

"Yep, she's got kidney stones," the vet declares on his way back in, film in hand. He slaps the x-ray up to a light panel on the wall and shows us the little white dots that represent the problem. He describes the surgery.

I have a question. "The operation is to her bladder?"

"Yes," Dr. Mom answers for him as if it's obvious.

"Yes, the kidney looks fine. Stones often develop in the bladder instead," he says.

I shoot her a look. It's a perfectly valid question. After all, they aren't called *bladder* stones.

But she's not to be silenced. He gives instructions for the twice a day painkiller to be given orally with a little syringe.

"Is there another way?" she asks.

"Well, there's a pill, but I figured you didn't want that ... given the wheelchair," he says.

"Even the syringe is going to be hard," my mom says. "See, she lives alone and has ataxia." Then, realizing he probably has no idea what that means, "She shakes a lot. It acts almost like cerebral palsy."

I cut her off then, before she can go on. "Mom, can you just come over and do it?"

Once we're in the parking lot, I let loose. "It's nothing like cerebral palsy!"

"I said it *acts* like cerebral palsy."

"Right. And you have no idea what you're talking about!"

Having a handicapped daughter makes her an expert on handicaps? She's never even met a person with cerebral palsy. I have and they'd probably be just as offended as I am. Cerebral palsy is probably the only handicap she knew the name for. I fume during the silent drive home.

It's weeks later and Bella's surgery is over. I ask Kris to administer the morning syringe during our workout sessions so my mom only has to come over in the evening. She gave me a sincere apology twice for the cerebral palsy comment.

Bella's stitches are out, and the stones are gone, but she's still peeing outside her litter box. She just squats on the floor and goes right in front of me. The vet says there's no medical reason for it. It's like she got used to the tile and likes it better than getting her feet all sandy. She must not think my life is challenging enough without attempting to clean up cat pee under a desk.

While I'm down there cleaning and reaching till I'm about to fall out of the wheelchair, the phone rings. I hit my head on the desk on the way back up. It's my doctor's office. They want me to "just swing by" for another urinalysis. I turn my head to see Bella squatting in a different corner of the office. Yellow liquid pools beneath her and starts running along the grout lines of the tile. My sentiments exactly.

ON THE FARM

Arguments with my mother can sound like Abbott and Costello routines. We park in the car, and she prepares to take Frankie out to do his business.

"When we get back, we can eat!" she tells him.

"I thought you said you didn't bring any cookies," I say.

"I didn't. You said you brought grapes."

"I did. But those are for lunch."

"But we always have a snack at the park."

"Yes. We always have cookies. You're welcome to the grapes. But they were for lunch."

"Well, I didn't bring cookies. I thought we could eat your grapes."

"Again. We can. I'm just saying, they were for lunch."

Frankie whimpers to remind us he needs to go out or this could go on forever. As the door shuts, she shoots me a look that says I'm a spoiled child, unwilling to share.

We're at the same park we stop at every Saturday in Woodbine, Georgia. It's another 15 minutes to our destination, Palmetto Oaks Stable, and my weekly therapeutic horseback riding session.

We're definitely in rural Georgia. Before the park, there's a sign that reads, "Dead Peoples Things For Sale." Umm. Where I come from, we call that an estate sale.

When my mom and Frankie return to the car, there is no mention of grapes. I'm relieved. I don't like feeding Frankie people food. My mother will give him a bite of her steak and then wonder why he begs.

Of the two of us, I'm the disciplinarian. He's much better than when I first started walking him. I use the word "come" now, instead of "snack." I taught him all the basic commands. He even rolls over. That one takes two hands to teach, one to hold the treat close to his nose and one to guide him over. So I only got him halfway there. For a while, whenever I said "rollover," he flopped on his back with all four feet in the air. Kris stepped in to help me. Trouble is, now he rolls over at every command. "Sit," "down," "shake," the words don't matter to him. It's his best trick and he knows it, so he throws it in whenever he can.

We turn onto the dirt road leading to the stable and see several trucks parked next to the woods backing up to Teresa's property. Two men wearing bright orange vests are talking. Hunters. Teresa, the stable owner and riding instructor, saw an adult deer with two spotted fawns just weeks ago. As we pass the men, I say a little prayer for the deer's safety and for some minor Dick Cheney incident to deliver its swift karmic justice.

Frankie's excitement nears epic proportions as we drive through the gate. We roll down the windows so he can take in the scent, and I hang on to him by his harness. He's a bright dog, but I think he'd jump right out if he could.

"Where's Sassy? Where is she?" Mom and I ask him. He looks around wildly, hopping from the center console to my lap, to the window and back.

Sassy is Teresa's dog and Frankie's buddy. They tear around the farm together until Frankie collapses somewhere. Sassy's mix of Shitzu and Jack Russell Terrier means that she will always outrun Frankie. His energy comes in short, quick bursts, while hers is more sustained. When she finally needs to cool off, she picks a stream, while Frankie, who hates water, prefers to wallow in a big pile of mud.

I call the place a farm, but the only animal aside from Sassy and the eight horses is Alice the goat. Alice is all black and the fattest goat I've ever seen. She looks the way a kid would draw any four-legged animal -- a big oval atop little stick legs. Aside from whatever goats usually eat , Alice loves junk food. And there are plenty of children willing to share their Cheetos.

The minute we park, Frankie bounds from the car. Alice takes one look at us and heads for the barn. Last week, she made the mistake of running when Frankie already had her in his sight. There is little he loves more than a good chase. Alice hoofed it clear across an arena and a large field and was heading for the woods before Frankie ran out of gas. I was a little worried as it unfolded, but Teresa just said, "I didn't know Alice could run that fast."

My mom pushes my wheelchair down a dirt path, struggling as we bump over tree roots, until Teresa comes to pull from the opposite end. Teresa is a few years younger than my mom and has good strength and agility due to running the place. Her short, reddish hair is shoved up under a ball cap. They make their way up a steep ramp until I am level with the horse's back. Carrie, a 15-year-old volunteer, has brought out Thunder for me to ride. I stand up with my mom and Teresa holding either arm. Carrie holds the horse as I swing my right leg over, using my left hand to grab the saddle horn. I'm on.

It still amazes me that this simple act, which used to be second nature to me, is such effort now. You would think walking, or rather not walking, would strike me this way. After all, walking is a far simpler and more natural act. And yet, in the moments after I have worked hard to walk a mere 20 feet with Kris, I don't think about how easy it used to be. This, on the other hand, hits me fresh. I miss riding a horse more than walking.

We head to the obstacle arena to practice the routine for the show. There's an end of year horse show in a couple of weeks. All the students will ride and prizes will be awarded. Most of the riders have cerebral palsy or autism. I'm the only one who had a stroke. I'm also the oldest rider by more than 20 years. I'm not sure why that is. Do adults give up and accept their fate? Stop living? Then again, I was often the oldest able-bodied rider, too. Maybe horseback riding is like ballet lessons or piano or soccer. Most people explore these things when they're young. Then they either give them up or get serious. Children and family take priority. But I still indulged my varied interests well into my thirties. I planned on becoming fluent in Spanish until even English became a challenge.

I'm sure I'm making progress, and the benefits of riding as therapy are undeniable, but really I just wanted to be on a horse again.

I've been riding over a year now, and I've graduated from two side-walkers (who walk along each holding a leg) to just Teresa on my right side. Carrie leads the horse and has moved from a short lead to a long lead, to often no lead, leaving me fully in charge of directing the horse.

After I practice the routine for the show, we head to the other arena. Sometimes I play catch with Carrie, who tosses an over-sized ball to me on the horse. Other times I work at my fine motor control, grabbing rings or other small objects to place on a pole or in a basket.

But today I work on standing up in the stirrups. This is good for me. I am weight-bearing. Something I'm not, most of the time. I'm returning to the saddle with quivering thighs when I hear Carrie.

"Eeewww. That's disgusting."

I follow her gaze to where Frankie is sitting before a large pile of horse manure, scarfing it up. He throws his head back, choking it down, as if at any moment the magnificent delicacy might be taken away.

"Frankie!" I am mortified.

He stops. He glances at me before returning to his meal. This is all the authority he deigns to grant me.

"Frankie! *Come,*" I command in as low a voice as I can manage. He ignores me, eating faster.

It's futile. I'm stuck on a horse. Carrie and Teresa can't leave me. And even if they could, they are laughing too hard to be of any assistance. Frankie can polish off the entire mound, and there's nothing I can do about it.

Then it occurs to me. Where is my mother in all this?

I glance back across the ring and see her seated, reading a book.

"Mother."

She looks up. "What?"

"Can you get Frankie? He's eating horse shit,"

She shrugs. She's the picture of Zen. I turn back to Frankie to scream, "No!"

I hear her call feebly, "C'mere Frankie. Snack!" Frankie doesn't even glance up.

Snack? She's calling snack? He's got an entire field full of snacks. He's in line at the all-you-can-eat buffet and not about to give up his place for some dry dog biscuit.

I turn back to her. Here I am, about to fall off the horse for yelling, and she doesn't even get out of her chair.

"I can't control him. There's no use getting upset about it," she says. More life lessons, courtesy of AA. She's co-dependent no more. Maybe it's just me, but I don't think that applies here. You should be able to control a dog.

Later, we are in the car on our way home. Frankie had returned to sit by my mom after having his fill. I take out the wet wipes and prepare for our lunch. Frankie's curled up on a towel in the backseat, too full and exhausted to beg. If this were the comics, there'd be squiggly fume lines coming from him like Pig Pen from "Peanuts." He stinks. He should be followed around by that dirty dust cloud, too. My mom will put him straight in the tub when we get home. He only gets the professional grooming treatment once a month. A take off on Versace, Fursace even has designer dog sweaters. I imagine folks lined up around the block, based on name alone.

We pass the hunters on our way out. They're returning to their trucks after what appears to be an unsuccessful day. I smile.

I take out the ziplock bag of grapes and hold it out to my mom.

"You brought grapes?" She smirks. "Imagine that."

SHE GETS IT

It's dark except for the lights coming from the noisy waterfront bars and the headlights of cars that bounce around us. People keep turning into the lot and filling up empty spaces. Lauren wheels ahead of me, behind the row of parked cars on our right, lit by the headlights of a passing car. It's 10:30 p.m. On a Saturday. Risky. It isn't just that it's late, and we're hard to see. Half these drivers are probably drunk, too.

"We're gonna die!" I holler to Lauren, who laughs as she wheels, looking in all directions. I concentrate on the two feet of road in front of me and on keeping the distance to Lauren the same. I don't want to lose her, nor do I want to run into the back of her chair.

I'm driving my power chair, as I often do with Lauren. She's the one friend who never pushes me. Also in a wheelchair, Lauren was partially paralyzed in a car accident almost 18 years ago. Divorced with two grown kids in college, she moved to Jacksonville about six months ago with the warm, friendly manner of someone eager to make friends. She became my first close disabled friend. Until Lauren, I didn't know how much I needed one.

"We're not going to die." She laughs as we arrive at her van. I breathe a huge sigh of relief, but her smile has faded. Someone's parked too close. Her van has a ramp that slides out, allowing us to get in. There's a sticker on her window that says not to park within eight feet, but no one ever reads that. It happens all the time. We're stuck.

"I'll get Kathy," she says and rolls back into the restaurant while I wait. Kathy is the caregiver and friend of another woman we know, Diana, who was diagnosed with MS some 20 years ago. Kathy and Diana often give me rides, and I've been swimming in their pool several times. They introduced me to Lauren one night during an adaptive bowling outing with the group from Sunns. Close in age, Lauren and I became fast friends.

Lauren returns with Kathy, who backs up the van, blocking the street. The ramp unfolds, and Kathy jumps out.

"What would we do without you?" I ask. It's my way of thanking her, but I know Lauren would've asked a stranger to move her car. She isn't shy. Her assertive nature is one of the things I like about her.

We wish Kathy "Happy Birthday" and say goodnight.

When we arrive at my house, Lauren waits while I fumble with my keys. "I'll pick you up at 12:30," she yells from the window. We're going to lunch the next day.

Another thing I like about Lauren is that she enjoys eating out as much as I do. We've tried all kinds of restaurants: seafood, Italian, Mexican, Greek. I'm braver with her than with able-bodied people. You'd assume the opposite. After all, I can hop curbs or be pushed out of trouble by an able-bodied person. But I'm so careful and conscious of being a burden, that I take few risks. With Lauren, I'm free to be my adventurous self.

Like when we tried a Japanese restaurant and discovered the ramp to the front door too steep. I had to use my power chair to tow Lauren in her manual chair. She hung on to the back of my chair while I pulled her up and around a long, rickety-looking bridge over what were supposed to be Japanese gardens and a koi pond, but just looked like muddy water and a bunch of weeds. Once inside, the stench of filthy mop water greeted us, along with a hostess who looked grateful to have something to do. When the handicapped bathroom stall was only big enough to pull straight in, not shut the door, that was all the excuse we needed. We mumbled our apologies and left without ordering, saving our laughter and disbelief for the car. On the way out and down the ramp of death, Lauren again had to be towed, this time using my power chair as a brake to keep her from flying at top speed into the parking lot. An able-bodied friend would've just left me in the car and run in to assess the place. It's more work with Lauren, but more fun, too.

One of my favorite things about our friendship is that I don't feel I'm putting her out or always asking for favors. I am getting rides. She drives, and I don't. That much is a fact. But it seems I never have to ask -- she always anticipates. Maybe it stems from being handicapped, but it isn't like that with able-bodied friends. An invitation isn't just an invitation with Lauren. It's an invitation *with* transportation. And that's so much better.

We're friends on a more level playing field. Although Michele and Jen will offer to help, the very fact that they end up doing so leaves me feeling obligated and indebted to them in a way I don't feel with Lauren. On a shopping outing, while other friends lug the wheelchair in and out of the trunk, pushing me and trying to balance clothes and store bags, Lauren and I roll right in and ask for help.

Not always, though. Like me, Lauren values her independence and has a taste for adventure. She prefers to try to figure things out before looking for assistance. Before she got her van, when I would take my manual chair, she tried to get that chair in the back of her

SUV for a half-hour before she finally acquiesced and let me call a neighbor.

Having been disabled a much longer time, Lauren's picked up a lot of knowledge. She's advised me on navigating Medicare, traveling disabled and repairing a wheelchair.

But best of all, having a disabled friend means having someone who really gets it. As close as I am to other friends, there's a part of me now they just can't relate to, a part of me they'll never understand.

I'm on the phone with Lauren the night before a big garage sale that I'm hosting. Lucy, Michele and my mom are all coming over and bringing things to sell from my driveway.

"Stay in the back. Don't let people see you unless you want to be the topic of conversation," Lauren warns.

I don't listen to her. And I pay for it. All day I have strangers asking questions, children staring, and my mother having conversation after conversation about what a miracle I am. By the end of the day, I have a headache and sore cheeks from too much fake smiling.

"I told you so!" Lauren can't resist saying on the phone later that night.

"What is so intriguing about a person in a wheelchair?" I rant. "Everybody had to know my story. And they weren't asking me. Everyone was talking to my mom about me. I'm surprised she didn't get tired of it all. And I'm definitely tired of hearing myself referred to in the third person."

"Does she need to have a drink?" Lauren asks.

"Who? Huh?" I ask. And then laugh. "Very funny. Yes, she does."

"Be there soon," she says.

I hang up my phone with a grin. She gets it.

REGRET

Today is my father's 70th birthday. Debbie threw him a surprise party and I'm not there. I feel bad about that. There were all kinds of justifiable reasons why I didn't go, but the bottom line is I didn't. My absence will be palpable.

For starters, I didn't want to go. All those people who know me, but I don't know them. It's the same way with a lot of my mom's friends. The only child holds a special place. You're The Daughter. But friends of your parents are just people. Maybe they haven't seen me since I was little. I know they haven't seen me in the wheelchair. Someone would have come up to me just as I managed to take a bite. All that small talk, with food on my face or spitting something. No, I probably wouldn't have eaten at all, just to be safe. And then everyone would say, "Oh, aren't you eating?" I always want to respond, "Yeah? You try eating on your lap in nice clothes with one shaky hand." But of course, I don't because those people are just being nice, making conversation. They don't know what a hassle it is.

I used to be good at that stuff. Eating and drinking and mingling. Talking to strangers. People would say, "Oh Pete, this is your daughter? She's so pretty/smart/sweet." And he'd look at me all proud and joke, "Yeah, she turned out okay in spite of me."

My dad's 93-year-old aunt went to the party. She made the trip from Miami with cousins and is probably sitting there in her wheelchair, a highball in her own shaky hand. She's half blind and well on her way to deaf, so what's my excuse? All I can say is that when you're old, people expect it. I'm more of a tragedy.

We would've been parked next to each other, conversation lagging. The people pushing us would have already made the joke about having wheelchair races. Of all the unoriginal things to say. I don't know why people think that's funny. It's right up there with motorboat noises in my book. But put two people pushing wheelchairs together, and someone can't resist the comment.

My great aunt Eileen and I used to have plenty to say to each other. Whenever we were at one of those family gatherings, she'd sidle up to me and ask, "So, how's your love life?" And I'd regale her with tidbits from the latest drama. Then she'd assure me there was still plenty of time. I stopped hearing about my plethora of time around age 30. It seems time starts to run out then. She stopped asking about my love life after the hemorrhage. I was no longer expected to have one. Honestly, it was a relief. I was knocking on the door to 40. In my aunt's heyday, I wouldn't have just been an old maid, I'd have been a dead one. It's a sad commentary on society when disability is a welcome substitute for the stigma of being unmarried and 40.

My dad's environmental friends are there, too. Pretty much everyone there who's not family has something to do with nature. My dad and stepmother were married in a swamp if that tells you anything. A wildlife preserve in Martin County set among Native American artifact mounds. It was the first time I was a bridesmaid. Debbie and I wore long, colorful skirts made by Seminole Indians and walked down a boardwalk toward my father in his Seminole jacket. Thousand-year-old cypress trees stood in attendance with their knobby knees and branches that dripped Spanish Moss.

My dad's been an environmentalist his whole life. Debbie runs the Hobe Sound Nature Center in the small South Florida town where they live. All their friends and colleagues have something to do with that world. Even in his early teaching days, my dad taught Biology and Environmental Science. He used to take his students seining in the grass flats and mangroves of Matheson Hammock near Biscayne Bay. An old photo shows me as a toddler, squatting in the sand, examining a shell and delighting in the animal inside. He taught me early on that things like sand dollars were alive even when they didn't appear to be.

My love for animals and the outdoors comes from him. During the summers throughout junior high and high school, I stayed with him and worked as day camp counselor and "turtle scout" for the Nature Center. The Center hosted programs about sea turtles for the public and late night walks on the beach to see them lay their eggs. The turtle scouts walked in pairs looking for the nesting females, then radioed back to Debbie at the pavilion that it was okay to bring the group; the turtle was laying her eggs. Once she starts, she won't stop. Even with all those people watching. My dad still rides an ATV early each summer morning to count the crawls and nests. He identifies the type of turtle by its tracks and files a report. He works as an independent contractor now, but I think he'd do it for free.

There are two other photos I love. In one, he and I are at the Grand Canyon, our backs to the camera, looking at the wide expanse in front of us. I wish I remembered it, but I was only three or four. All I remember is the parking lot where I fell on broken glass and needed stitches.

The other photo is an old newspaper article that my mother had framed. The picture is of my dad and me paddling a canoe, my 10-year-old self swallowed up by a life jacket, the headline, "His Canoe Trip Carries Message." My dad canoed the waterways around the state of Florida to raise awareness and publicity for coastal conservation. He camped and stayed with different locals, giving the bow seat of certain legs of the trip to various legislators, government representatives or news reporters. I went with him for 100 of the 1000-mile journey. I remember it as my introduction to Spam and finding a baby turtle I carried with us, then released.

It's hard to imagine my parents ever together, but looking at that picture, I can see what my mother saw in him. He's young, younger than I am now, with gray just beginning to pepper his sideburns and beard. And he's thinner than I ever remember seeing him. He looked like Ernest Hemingway. My mom says he opened up a whole new world to her. Taught her things she never knew. About nature and wildlife and untamed places.

I'd phoned him earlier this morning to wish him a happy birthday, but he wasn't born till just before midnight New Year's Eve. He missed being one of the New Year's babies by less than ten minutes. My grandma missed out on a lot of free diapers. He was in the car with his brother-in-law when I called. They were going fishing. Fly fishing.

"Dad, you know how to fly fish?"

"Daughter, I was fly fishing back when you were in diapers."

How did I not know this? All I know about fly fishing is from *A River Runs Through It,* and it seemed like an art form. He doesn't know books or movies, but this he knows. He knows how to do everything. He *is* like Hemingway. Only without the writing or the drinking. Oh, and he would never hunt. My dad could never shoot anything. An animal suffering is worse. I remember him hitting a squirrel when I was visiting one summer. I was in the back seat with my younger step-cousins. Being boys, they immediately looked back while I kept my gaze straight ahead.

"Don't worry, Uncle Pete. You didn't kill it. It limped off," one of them said.

I saw the anguish in his eyes in the rear-view mirror.

I got off the phone that morning, saying I had to walk Frankie. If I had gone to the party, it would have been a great lie to throw him off course. As it was, I'd told the truth.

Another reason I didn't go was my aunt's bad back. She was my ride down, and I didn't want her lifting the wheelchair. Then I found out my step-cousin Dan and his new wife, Julia, were driving from Jacksonville, but they were staying two nights. I decided against the expense of a hotel. The wheelchair doesn't fit in my dad's older house. I didn't want to spend the holiday alone in a hotel room anyway. Traveling and being away from home is a big deal now.

The clock on the microwave reads 4:36. The party is over. I pick up my cell again and dial his number.

"Well, hello again, daughter!"

"Were you surprised?" I ask.

"Yep. She pulled it off."

"I'm sorry I didn't make it down."

"You were missed. A lot of people asked about you."

He thanks me for the present. I hang up the phone. It's dark out. I look at the newspaper article framed above my desk. His hair is all white now. And he's heavier. He hurt his knee last summer on the ATV. He can't do everything anymore.

The house is quiet. My mom picked up Frankie earlier. Outside on the street, someone is shooting off a few early fireworks. My gift to him was a watch. It's supposed to be for everyday, but he'll probably think it's too nice to wear on the boat.

I could have paid for the hotel instead.

I let my handicap stop me.

I should have gone.

I ♥ MY POMEGRANATE

My mom's a little ditzy. I used to think our miscommunications were my fault because of my voice. Not anymore. It's not just me. She can be spacey. And hard of hearing. Not that she'd ever admit it.

She's quick to point out when I'm slurring worse than usual. She thinks she's figured it out. That it's tied to my energy. It's true that everything, including my voice, is worse when I'm tired, but being tired isn't always the answer. One day, for example, I wasn't a bit sleepy, yet I repeated myself every other sentence. It was exhausting.

"You're tired, aren't you?" she asked.

I felt like a three-year-old who's been busted rubbing her eyes and knows she's going to be put down for a nap. "Just tired of repeating myself."

Okay, so I was cranky, too.

I had already endured my mother fighting with some guy over a handicapped parking place, and I hate conflict. Unless I'm the one who's yelling. Then I like it.

But that day, it was my mother. I should have known what was coming when she slowed, passing the space, as she always does, checking for a permit. (Apparently, someone made her the permit police.) There wasn't one. Not hanging off the rearview mirror, not on the license plate. She learned to check the plate after barking at some woman who barked right back, "Check the license tag before you go getting all high and mighty with me!"

High and mighty. That's exactly how she gets. Meanwhile, I always keep my mouth shut. Mom leaps in with enough force for both of us. I suppose it stems back to her activist days. She's never minded jumping into the fray.

I, on the other hand, don't fancy the face-off. Years ago, protesting the circus, I stood at the entrance handing out flyers, trembling like a timid Chihuahua the whole time. I left early and swore never again.

So this SUV without a permit is parked in the handicapped spot at our hair salon. Mom leaves me on the sidewalk and walks right into the realty office in front.

Oh, Lord. Here we go. Inside, I see her pointing to me. She's having words with some guy at a desk. Oh, brother. They're coming outside, his keys in hand.

"There was nobody here," he says, like that makes a difference.

"We're here now," Mom says.

"Sorry," the man huffs. He isn't. I'm embarrassed, but a little proud, too.

And then she blows it.

"Don't do it again," she says. This is just too much for his ego to handle.

"Look lady. You don't have to be so rude."

"Rude? *I'm* rude?"

Just then my hairdresser, Jill, opens the door.

"What's going on?" she asks me over the yelling.

"Just pull me in," I say.

Once inside, Jill mixes color as my mother plops in a swivel chair. "Ugh. That guy was way out of line," she says. "Just give me a second to decompose."

I look at my mother, then at Jill, who has stopped mixing, confused. She looks at me. We burst out laughing.

"What?" my mother asks.

I'm still laughing, but Jill manages, "Well, we're all decomposing a little every day." This only makes me laugh harder.

My mother is still puzzled, looking back and forth between the two of us.

"You mean *decompress*?" I ask, still laughing.

At least she's starting to acknowledge the problem -- this propensity to use the wrong word. She'll substitute a word without missing a beat. Like last week. She confessed she was out walking Frankie, a Pekingese, when the name of his breed escaped her.

"What kind of dog is that?" some passerby asked.

"A Pomegranate," said my mother, without hesitation.

After the decomposing issue, I suspected our misunderstandings might have more to do with some less-than-quick wit on her part than any speech impediment on mine.

During one phone conversation, she told me she would pick me up at eight a.m. I responded that I had every faith in the world she would be on time. It's kind of a running joke of ours since she's not exactly a morning person.

"You have every what?" she asked.

"Faith."

"Tape?"

"F as in Frank," I started to spell.

"What about Frank?"

My suspicions were validated one day when friends from Miami visited. I was on the phone with her when, in the background, I heard one of them ask if he could turn on the oven. "We're going to make strawberry pies," he said.

"What?" asked my mother.

"We're going to make strawberry pies."

"Strawberry ties?"

"No. *Pies.*"

"Ohhh. I was going to say ..." she trailed off.

"We're going to make strawberry *pies,*" he repeated. "Why would I say strawberry ties, Suzanne? That doesn't even make sense."

Exactly. I know if I was losing my hearing and didn't want to admit it, my common sense would be working double time to fill in the blank. Not so with my mother.

We ended up going out to lunch that day after the hair salon. At the restaurant, I apologized for my bad mood.

"Baboons?"

"Yes, baboons, Mom. I'm apologizing for my baboons."

She's looking at me, confused. It's amazing how you can want to protect someone and strangle her at the same time. But I don't strangle her. I just take a deep breath. All I need is a second to decompose.

GEEZ LOUISE!

I've become crotchety before my time. In the space of a half mile, I've complained about the loud base vibrating in the car behind us and asked my mom to turn down the music. The young man walking down the street is the final straw. "Oh, come on!" I holler, even though the windows are up. "Pull your pants up!"

"Okay, old lady," my mom says.

"Well, gimme a break. That's ridiculous. They're halfway down his butt! He's tripping, see? He's gonna fall on the concrete!"

"Okay, calm down. God, I'm more hip than you, and I'm the senior citizen."

She's right. I use the terms "Holy Moly" and "Lord have mercy" on a regular basis. I have no idea what 3G and 4G are except that they have to do with cell phone features that I may or may not have. And when we watched *Entertainment Tonight* last week, I didn't know who anyone was. "Who's that kid everyone's flipping out over?" I asked.

"Justin Bieber. *Everyone* knows that."

"Well, for God's sake, what is he, *twelve*?"

I'm not hip, in part, because I'm a homebody by nature. It's kind of expected. Everyone understands why I stay at home when it rains. Being handicapped means always having the perfect excuse for getting out of something. These days, I don't do anything I don't want to do. It's fabulous. And true! Though, as my mom is quick to point out, "You could always just say no, thank you." Another tip from the AA toolbox -- how to set boundaries. But despite my introverted inner self, I can't deny the entire aging process is being sped up by my handicap.

I have more in common with old people now. Those who need some type of mobility aid to get around -- a walker, wheelchair or cane. After all, we share the same parking places and bathroom stalls. Just the other day, my bus driver helped a woman with her walker. I watched him place it on the street for her, at the bottom of a curb. *Lord, put it on top of the curb,* I thought. She must have said that very thing, because he nodded and moved it. I think about these things now. One man's curb is another man's Everest.

I used to get antsy behind any slow-moving senior. At the register, an ATM, any line. Stepping up too close, shifting my weight side to side. Now I have infinite patience. In fact, it's more likely someone's waiting on *me*. My mother, in her quest for meaning, thinks the hemorrhage happened to teach her patience.

She's restless, exasperated. I can see her fighting the urge to say, *C'mon already!* when I put my eyeglasses in their case, then take out, clean and fumble with my sunglasses. Or when she waits for me to get in the Jeep while I position my wheelchair to transfer, setting each brake and placing each foot. But what can she say? I'm doing my best, and she knows it. But it's not a speedy process, that's for sure.

She'd have done well in a fast-paced city, like Manhattan, bustling along the sidewalk at breakneck speed. One should never say never, so I'll say I'd be surprised if I ever return there now that I'm disabled. I just can't see making it there. Besides being pretty inaccessible, I imagine being trampled on the sidewalk or running over toes with my power chair in an effort to keep up. No, I'm perfectly at home in Florida, land of power scooters. There's something about the South that slows everyone down, like the beaches remind people of being on vacation.

My grandma and I are tight now. I pass along all my disability catalogs to her. She couldn't believe all the great products they have in *Disabled World*. And one could go crazy in the *Sammons-Preston* catalog, which is basically a big Handicaps-R-Us.

Our new relationship was first forged when I had a special toilet seat delivered to my aunt's house for my visits. The special seat attached to the existing one, adding an extra three inches of height. Big, removable handles on either side made it easy to transfer, but I found them most helpful in not falling off.

My grandma coveted that toilet seat. My aunt moved it into my grandmother's bathroom after I went home. When I heard this, I bought a second toilet seat to give her as a present. For Christmas, no less. You know you're old when you tear (or in her case carefully unfold) the wrapping and squeal with delight over a toilet seat. And I, a good 50 years younger, knew just how she felt.

My grandma and I have lots to talk about now. We commiserate over how difficult and time-consuming it is to take a shower. We both prefer the bigger peel and stick address labels you can actually get your fingers under. And she makes a very convincing argument for the appeal of the housedress. I gave serious thought to something in one of my catalogs called the Granny Jo Bath Cape.

For being in her nineties, my grandmother is quite impressive. She answers the *Jeopardy!* questions before most contestants can even hit their buzzers. She pedals two miles a day on her tricycle.

And her penmanship is so neat and small, I'm the one reading her letters with a huge magnifying glass. There are some good genes in the family.

My grandma and I gravitate toward each other at family functions. We both stare at the hummus and pita chips and decide against them. There's no way I can handle them without leaving crumbled chips in the dip and hummus on my face. And she wrinkles her nose at anything more exotic than a ham sandwich and a glass of milk.

While I used to sit with cousins my age, now I sit next to my grandma, so she can cut my string beans. She's thrilled.

Allowing myself to be taken care of in this fashion is fine in the privacy of Aunt Eileen's or Cousin Boyd's. But out in public, I try to retain a fraction of cool-ness, the degree of which has diminished over time. I'm happy to have the extra plastic sporks or super long straws at home. I just don't want to have the waiter track down extras, so my grandmother can stash them in her purse.

At our family's most recent dinner out, my grandmother tried to put a bib on me after tying one around her own neck. I shook my head, brushing her off, in essence denying our alliance. Embarrassed, I sat there with a look I hoped said, *Don't be silly! I don't need a bib.* And of course, I do. Anyone can look at my stained shirts and tell that. The floor beneath our table looked like a family just left with a two-year-old. One of the staff brought out the floor sweeper while another looked for the high chair to put away.

I'm an oxymoron. I can't wait to be old enough to live in a seniors-only community, yet staunchly oppose public bib-wearing. I think it's called ego. Maybe you get to a certain age and don't care how it looks -- you just want clean clothes.

My mother would rather live alone till the day she dies, her body found days later by the pest-control guy, than live in "one of those places." Not me. On the short bus just last week, we took someone home to Cypress Village, an adult community near my neighborhood. "Geez Louise!" I exclaimed. "Will you look at those sidewalks!"

They were wide and flat. Everywhere. There wasn't a curb or step in sight. Nirvana. Smooth, flat trails curved through pretty, wooded areas. According to my fellow passenger, there were independent houses, assisted living condos, a nursing home. A place for every stage of life. There were dining options, a salon, even a bank. I imagined myself trekking everywhere on my motorized wheels. And best of all, I'd be a common sight instead of a novelty.

Cypress Village is a world unto itself. That world may not appeal to everyone, but when you're disabled and don't drive, convenience moves pretty high up on the list of priorities.

I love living alone and doing things myself, but it's hard work. I've realized why my time seems to evaporate. Because it takes me 45 minutes to grab and eat a yogurt, after cleaning up the one I grabbed and spilled. Because emptying the cat litter and taking it out to the garbage is an activity fraught with tension and the potential for flying kitty poo. And because doing the laundry is a chore best spread out over several days. Even as I write this, clothes grow mildew in the washer from a load I started last week.

There's only one problem with the plan for my future and my dream of enjoying some easier living during my twilight years. Money.

Cypress Village or any community of its caliber isn't cheap at around $1,400 a month. I can always hope that my dad's been socking it away or my uncle's use of that antique mower has led to some fat bank account I don't know about. But chances are some government-assisted brick building that smells bad is in my future. It scares me. Maybe I should've had kids.

My mom and I sit, waiting to have our hair done. She's looking at a *People* magazine. "I have no idea who these people are," she says. I take the magazine from her and *Ooh! I know this one!*

"That's Kristen Stewart," I say smugly. "You know, the *Twilight* movies?"

"Oh," she shrugs, above it all.

Just then, a twenty-something walks in and kisses his wet-haired girlfriend. "Hey, babe," he says. He's wearing a baseball cap backward and his shorts hang low, too low, on his hips.

I look up at my mother who's shooting me a look that says to be quiet. As if I'd say something. He's wearing headphones anyway, and talking to somebody on his phone. He probably has 5G. I sigh. Kids these days.

DOWNHILL IN A BUCKET

I look over the mountain from my little perch inside the bucket. I'm sitting cozy in my ski gear, my legs covered with extra blankets. Skiers and snowboarders swish all around me. I'm a huge, immobile rock in the fast flow of the river. From up here, the people are colorful moving dots that cover the mountainside, clustering at the bottom by the ski lift. I feel J.P. push on my bucket, lining it up. "Ready?" he yells through the icy wind. The only parts of me completely warm are my ears, inside the helmet.

"Yeah," I yell back, but inside I'm not so sure. I can't see him, but I know he's back there with my friend, Tracy. I remind myself it's his job to keep me safe. He's been doing this for years.

I feel my stomach dive as he gives the bucket a quick shove to send me out, over the flat ledge and down. And we're off.

The correct term for my "bucket" is bi-ski. It has rigid plastic that forms a seat and supports my back. My legs extend out in front of me, making the whole thing a bit like driving a super flimsy go-cart with no steering and no way to control it. My arms rest, useless on a front bar while J.P. does all the steering with the long, bright orange tethers that connect me to him. The whole contraption totters on top of two skis while two outriggers, mini-skis on poles, fit through the bucket on either side to give it stability and keep it from falling over.

As I learned, there's more than one way to get a disabled person down a mountain. There are many, in fact, depending on the disability. There are either bi-skis, like mine, with fixed outriggers, or mono-skis, for those with better balance and upper-body control, who want to use the outriggers to pole and steer themselves. There is tubing, ski biking and even skiing with a walker-type device mounted onto the skis. I saw blind skiers, quadriplegics and amputees while I was there. Everyone made their way down the mountain.

Tracy knew her way around the equipment room of the NSCD (National Sports Center for the Disabled in Winter Park, Colorado), because she and her husband, Frank, lived just a short drive away, and both volunteered there. In fact, this whole trip had been her idea. I agreed to give it a shot as long as I could quit if I hated it. I thought it might be too painful, make me miss the joys of able-bodied skiing too much. I learned to ski in my thirties and loved it, taking five ski vacations before the hemorrhage.

When we entered the equipment room, it was abuzz with activity. People with a variety of challenges met their ski instructors and were fitted for equipment or were suiting up to face the cold. It had just stopped snowing, and I wondered, not for the first time, how people in wheelchairs got by in snowy states. They must have special snow tires, because Tracy and I struggled with my flat-terrain, Sunshine State wheels over the snow and ice.

Tracy and I agreed -- I lucked out when it came to ski instructors. Not that J.P. was the most capable or the most experienced. Maybe he was, I don't know. But he was definitely the cutest.

J.P. had mischievous green eyes that sparkled when he laughed at one of my jokes, told one of his own or skied. So pretty much all the time. He was several years younger than me and had a bald head which in no way detracted from his good looks. It was always covered by a ski cap anyway. He was an ex-baseball player, as evidenced by his strong physique and the way his cheek bowled out with a bolus of sunflower seeds. Every so often, he would expertly spit shells over the side of the ski lift.

"Leftover habit. These helped me quit," he explained with a sheepish grin as we approached the end of the lift for another run.

"Better than tobacco," I replied. He could do no wrong.

We got ready to dismount. Or should I say, J.P. and Art, another volunteer and instructor-in-training, got ready to dismount. I sat there. They reattached the section of the bi-ski that dangled when seated on the lift. Then, they each grabbed a side of the bi-ski and lifted me off at just the right moment, skiing on either side of me and pulling me away from the crowds. We waited for Tracy, who'd ridden in the lift behind us.

Tracy let Art step in to assist without hesitation. The lift made her nervous. She hadn't helped a live skier on or off the lift yet, but she and another volunteer had helped a sand-filled dummy during training and lost it down a hill. She told me the story on the drive up, how she and the other girl were about to head up the mountain and were trying to detach part of the sit-ski for the ride. Then, they failed to hoist their "skier" all the way onto the seat. The momentum from the chair lift sent the training dummy, decked out in full ski gear and helmet, skiing unmanned down a small slope. It came to a stop after falling over sideways. The crowd, believing it to be a real person, gasped. Things only quieted down after Tracy and her partner skied off and brought it back. After that story, I was glad Art was assisting, too.

By the third run down, two things had become apparent. That I had developed a mad crush on J.P. , and I loved adaptive skiing. There's still nothing like racing down the mountain on your own, reaching the bottom, heart pounding and sweaty beneath all that gear. But adaptive skiing has its benefits. Like speed. J.P. was a much better skier than I had ever been, so I traveled faster in my bucket than I ever had the nerve to go before. And there were no lines. Though I've refused to let my mom take me to Disney World to get ushered to the front of long lines, here I didn't mind skipping the wait. Plus, regular skiing is a lot of work. Getting those ski boots on and off, lugging skis and wrestling all that clothing. I still had wrestling to do, but I wasn't sticky with sweat or already tired.

I also discovered I wasn't completely without control of my buggy. The sit-ski turned with just the slightest tilt of my head. I learned to lean ever-so-slightly and to always look in the direction I wanted to go. As the day progressed, J.P. steered less and less and I took on more and more control. After one of our final runs when the wind picked up, chasing many skiers inside for hot toddies, J.P. commented that my grin stretched ear to ear. Since it hadn't been too crowded on the slopes, he'd let me steer more. "That time," I told him, "it really felt ... like skiing."

"That's the idea," he said, grinning back.

Tracy also developed a small crush on J.P. At one point in the afternoon, she stood next to him and looked over at me. We were trying to figure out how tall he was without asking him.

It didn't look good. Tracy was only 5'4", and though he was several inches taller than her, he was definitely shorter than me. It's ridiculous to me that this mattered. First, it wasn't like I'd be standing. And second, in what world was I living to think he would date me, anyway?

It's interesting to me, and I've mulled this over since the beginning of my journey into the disabled world. I've found myself demoted more than a few leagues, and yet my tastes remain way up the rungs. So unless I begin fishing in my own pond and become attracted to my new physical equivalent (which I do *not* see happening), then I'm destined to never have a boyfriend again. Luckily, I like cats.

And please don't give me all that mumbo-jumbo about the right person seeing past the physical and loving my great sense of humor and inner beauty and all that crap. I think women are more likely to do that than men, and I like men. I was 36 when I had the hemorrhage, and I know how the world works. And I say it usually starts with physical attraction, which leads to romantic love, which sets things spinning.

So Tracy and I resigned ourselves to just enjoying the afternoon with a cute boy instead of wooing him. Me, because he played in the major leagues, while I'd been traded to the minors, and her, because she was married and could only look anyway.

He seemed to enjoy our company, too. "I've met so many great people," he said and told us about the fun girl with Tourettes he'd helped last week. I wondered if he really meant fun -- or fun*ny*.

"I know it must be a horrible disease and not at all funny to have, but how did you not laugh?" I asked.

I really wanted to know. I know he's supposed to be professional and all, but there's something so funny about your companion screaming *Motherfucker!* at the jerk that just cut you off on the slopes.

"I did laugh. *Sometimes*," he said. "Mostly I tried not to, but it was hard because she would laugh. She knew she was inappropriate. And she was really cool."

I think I would've liked her.

Maybe I have a childish sense of humor, but I think cussing is really funny. That, and falling down. It's terrible, but when someone trips or misses the chair or walks into a wall, my first reaction is to crack up. And then I remember to ask if they're okay. It's really bad if they're not, but even if they're fine they glare at me for laughing. It's obvious that mine is the wrong response if there are good-in-a-crisis people present. You know, the kind of people who are quick to run and help?

Unfortunately, no one witnessed Tracy's fall except me. And I let out a loud guffaw. She slipped on the ice-covered sidewalk outside Walgreens after we said our goodbyes to J.P. I remembered to ask if she was okay through the open car window about the time she was struggling back to her feet, which I did through the kind of raspy laughing that sounded like I'd smoked for years. "Nice," she said to me.

At some point an older gentleman had come around the corner to find Tracy splayed out on the ice and me in the car, laughing away. He seemed about to come to her aid, shooting me a dirty look, but by then she was on her feet. She entered the car while I carried on, snickering and replaying the scene in my mind. "I'm bleeding!" she said indignantly, pulling up her jeans to inspect her leg. You could tell she was trying to be serious and mad at me, but a smile was beginning to form. This only set me off again.

"I'm sorry! I know. It's terrible. I can't help it."

"Did you see that guy look at you? Probably wondering why you didn't get out to help me."

"I'm handicapped." I shrugged.

"Yeah, that's why."

When Tracy pushed me to the airport gate days later, I hugged her goodbye. My muscles hurt from laughing so much. My stomach felt all hollow with missing her already.

"Are you sure you guys won't move back to Florida?" I asked, knowing the answer.

"I doubt it. You move here. J.P. lives here," she added, nudging me with a playful elbow.

I rolled my eyes. She was a fan of the mumbo-jumbo, too. "I would have," I said, "before this." I gestured to the wheelchair.

"You could get snow tires."

I shook my head. "I think I'm settled."

Tracy passed me off to an airline attendant, who approached to wheel me through the gate. "Send the pictures!" I hollered back over my shoulder. But we were already moving away.

BECAUSE CURIOUS MINDS WANT TO KNOW

Everyone wants to know about sex. Can I and do I still have it? The answers are yes and no, respectively. A master at self-gratification at an early age and a sexually active adult, I wanted to be sure I hadn't lost the ability to star in my own one-woman show. So I reprised the role just the one time out of curiosity. Anything more than that would just be cruel. Fantasies about sex are like fantasies about walking or dancing or wearing high heels. It probably ain't gonna happen, so why torture myself?

I comfort myself in the knowledge of what Hemingway said about sex and writing. He said he eased off on making love when writing hard, as the two things were run by the same motor. I'm writing a best seller.

People think it's tragic that I was disabled in my prime. It is awful, to be sure, but not half as terrible as it would have been if I'd wanted a family. I hadn't yet met the one person with whom to spend the rest of my life. But as my mother is so gracious to point out, he might have left me anyway.

To be honest, I wasn't making any real progress on that front. At the time of the hemorrhage, I was dating a guy Viv and I nicknamed White Bread, because he was so boring he thought a plate of fried cheese was exotic. Had I ever taken him to my favorite sushi restaurant, he would have fallen over. And then he would have starved. I was 36 and still dating like I was on *Sex and the City*. There was always a deal breaker, and I was no Charlotte.

While on the fence about marriage, I was sure I didn't want kids. Not that I don't love kids. I do. Those belonging to others suit me just fine. I was quite close to Danielle's three boys before the hemorrhage. Now I'm not so sure. It's hard to bond with kids when you can't play with them. Instead of shooting hoops or mastering their video games, they're helping me zip up my jacket or fighting over who gets to play in the wheelchair.

I was nervous about seeing them for the first time post-hemorrhage. I didn't need to be. Kids are much more accepting of me in their world than adults. Although I don't know how Danielle explained things. Max, the youngest at four, told me upon parting to "feel better." Nick asked me how long the doctor said I have to be in the wheelchair. Regardless of their understanding, I think it's good for them to be around me. Maybe if more kids were exposed to people with disabilities, I wouldn't have to endure their constant stares.

Children are the worst about this. Most haven't yet been taught that it's impolite to stare. So while adults avoid eye contact, their children look at me like I have three heads. You haven't felt like crap until you smile at some kid, and he starts to cry. Now I just ignore them as they regard me with their big, doubtful eyes.

I've come to dread locations where kids gather. Malls, playgrounds, fast food restaurants -- I avoid them all. I've even been known to gun my power chair past a bus stop near my house while dragging poor Frankie, just so he won't stop. Show me a group of children, and I become an insecure 12-year-old.

I know it's innocent. I understand they're inquisitive. I still want them to cut it out.

"They're just being curious," my friend Tracy said. I refused to accompany her into a school to pick up her kids. "They're probably checking out the wheels. Kids love things with wheels, I don't know what is --"

"I'm not buying it," I said, but I allowed her to push me inside.

"Then stick your tongue out."

We laughed. "Is that what you tell your kids?" I asked.

I felt a lot better armed with a plan. I would stick my tongue out at the next saucer-eyed rugrat that eyeballed me. I would employ my inner grade schooler. Balance the seesaw, so to speak.

An unsuspecting little girl standing next to her mom fixated her wide eyes on me. "See?" I mouthed to Tracy.

"Do it," she said.

I stuck out my neck, bulged my eyes and pointed my tongue in her direction. She looked afraid for a second, then began tugging on her mom's arm. The woman looked down at her and the little girl pointed in my direction.

"Go, go go!" I said to Tracy.

She moved us down the hall as the woman looked in our direction. We hurried through the school's main corridor, weaving in and out of parents and children when we came to her son Ethan's classroom. He came out just as we were whizzing past. He raised his arms palms skyward as he watched us go. His bewildered expression read, *Where are you going?*

Tracy slowed down and turned us around. "Great," she said, out of breath. "What kind of an example am *I* setting?"

We approached Ethan.

"Honey," Tracy said. "You know it's impolite to stare, don't you?"

"Yes," he answered.

"And it's not nice to stick out your tongue," I added.

DINNER WITH FRIENDS

I'm feeling pretty good about myself as I wait for Laney and Ed at an outside table. It's warming up. At five o'clock, it's still bright enough to get away with sunglasses, so I look more normal than usual. I've managed to pull my power chair up to a table without running into it or sliding it over. The wine comes as requested, in a short glass with a straw. It's so easy to lift to my mouth, I don't have to bend down to the table with each sip, like the red, fluid-filled drinking duck my grandma used to own.

It's a big night in the neighborhood, the fifth anniversary of Art Walk. The once a month gathering when stores stay open late and live music fills the streets. Local artists set up stalls within a four block radius to showcase their merchandise.

Laney and Ed are a couple I met through Sunns. They're disabled and dating each other exclusively. They're about my age or a little younger, and like me, they each suffered a brain injury. Laney had a brain tumor removed and was left with ataxia, but still gets around with a walker. Watching her, I get a glimpse of how unsteady I must look, even in my wheelchair. It always looks like she's going to fall. You never know whether her limbs will go where she asks them to or somewhere else entirely. People watch and reach out to steady her.

She insists that she's fine. Only I believe her. It always looks worse than it is.

I know less about Ed's injury. It's not physical; he walks fine. It doesn't appear developmental or cognitive. He knows which end is up. In fact, to meet him, you might not guess he's disabled at all. Maybe it's his memory. I make a mental note to ask Laney someday and take another sip of wine.

They're late, but I don't care. I enjoy being out. The music, the wine, the promise of a good dinner.

"Amy? Hey!" a friend, Lori, walks up with another woman. Sliders Restaurant is a popular place on Thursday nights. Fish tacos and oysters during happy hour, not to mention all kinds of drink specials. It's getting crowded.

"Lori!" I say, delighted to see her. They've left their drinks at a large table. They're waiting on a group, but agree to sit for a moment. Lori introduces her friend and says the woman has published two children's books. We talk about writing and Lori's upcoming trip to Africa.

Laney and Ed approach when the two women leave, and I'm feeling popular. I should go out more often.

The waiter appears and takes their drink orders, tells us about the specials. It's dusk now, so I've switched to my regular glasses. Conscious of my wandering eye, I concentrate on looking at the left image of the waiter, so my eyes will appear straighter. I completely miss the specials.

It doesn't matter. When the time comes, I order what I always order. What I know I can handle without cutting assistance. Shrimp and grits. And a spoon. It's why I like returning to the same places. I've already cased the joint.

We're waiting on dinner, discussing the day's Blue Angels air show, when a tall man with a cane seesaws into my field of vision. I look up.

"Jeff?" I ask, though there's no question it's him. We all know each other from Sunns Adaptive Sports Program. We invite him to sit down, and he lowers himself into the empty chair next to me. The four of us look like an outing from the local adult daycare center. The waiter probably thinks the ladies at the next table are our chaperones.

It's weird, seeing Jeff out of context. Out socially.

"What are you doing at the beach?" I ask. He explains, with a mischievous grin, that he's here to meet a large group of ladies. When I ask how he managed that, he shakes his head to downplay it.

"A therapist at Sunns. You probably know her. Kim."

I shake my head. I don't.

"It's a bunch of her friends. I don't know them. I kind of invited myself."

"That's brave of you," I say. I'm a little impressed.

The waiter comes over to take Jeff's drink order. He orders water and scans the tables. "I don't see her." Laney keeps asking him to repeat himself. It's loud out here with the crowd and the music, but that's only part of the problem. Jeff talks like me, only he's a whole lot harder to understand. I gather he's had some kind of stroke, though I can't say for sure. There've been times at Sunns when I couldn't understand him, either, but tonight I'm not having a problem.

"He doesn't see her," I repeat for Laney. She nods. It's pretty bad when I'm the interpreter.

After ten minutes, our food arrives. "I think I've been stood up," Jeff says. "Good thing I ran into you guys."

I pass him a menu. "You should order." He does.

I have a heightened sense of awareness. The things I say. My table manners. I've done pretty well, except for the piece of food I spit across the table at Laney. Everyone pretended not to notice. Maybe they didn't.

It's loud enough to make talking across the table difficult. Laney and Ed's heads are bent in the intimate closeness of private conversation. Jeff and I have, likewise, talked mainly to each other. It's kind of nice. To be part of a couple sitting across from a couple. I didn't realize I'd missed it.

"There she is." He points to a large table. For a moment, I'm disappointed, then I remember he's already ordered. "I'm going to tell her it's too late. I found better company." He smiles.

He gets up and shuffles toward the big group. As soon as he's out of earshot Laney leans in. "You should hook up with Jeff."

I laugh. I haven't heard that term, or done anything like what it implies in years. Hook up. Disabled people don't "hook up." Young, attractive people unencumbered by canes and wheelchairs hook up. Not me. Not Jeff.

"Yeah, let me tell you how *that* would go."

"What?"

"*What?*"

"What?"

"*What?*" I take turns imitating each of us.

Jeff returns just as his dinner arrives. The conversation with Laney is over, but it's too late. The seed has been planted.

If I'm honest with myself, the thought already crossed my mind. Not "hooking up" per se, I still think that's ludicrous, but something akin to it. He's not a bad looking guy. I've always liked dark hair and eyes. And he's got one of my must-haves, as pointless as it is now

-- height. I sneak sideways glances at him and try to imagine what he looked like before his stroke. People who've had strokes tend to be physically changed. It could be something obvious, from speech or, like me, in the eyes, to something subtle like the way the lips and mouth move to form words. Something is off, not quite right, like watching a bad lip-syncher. Stroke survivors are a strange compilation of their past and present. Of what is and what was.

Ed finishes eating first. Laney and I are slowed down by our ataxia, so we finish right alongside Jeff, despite our head start.

When the take-home boxes arrive, Laney helps me. She's been out with me before.

She opens the box with a wagging hand and some fumbling. The other hand picks up my plate. "Can you do it?" I ask.

"I got it," she assures me. Then she tips the dish toward the box and the entire contents of my plate slide in a heap onto the table. We all laugh. The chaperones glance at us. The adult daycare group is having fun now.

As we prepare to leave, Kim the therapist comes over to say goodbye. Lori is behind her. Jeff makes introductions.

"I know you," Kim says to me. "I know her," she says to Jeff. "You're the writer."

As much as it pleases me to be The Writer, I have no idea who she is. This happens all the time. I've decided it's something that comes with the wheelchair. In it, I'm memorable. Everyone knows me. With my bad eyesight, they're lucky if I can see them, much less remember them.

Turns out they're all together. Kim and her friends are the very people that Lori was waiting on. Kim and I know a lot of the same people.

Since we're all leaving at the same time, we travel as one large group. Which is good for Jeff, who now has a foot in each party.

We proceed along the sidewalk, passing each booth. Large crowds are the great equalizer; matching the disabled and able-bodied, causing everyone to shuffle along at a 90-year-old's pace. There are even some 90-year-olds in the throng, happy for the company.

Everyone looks at the art and jewelry displays. Except me. After two glasses of wine, I am absorbed in not running over any toes, or worse, off the sidewalk, the edges blurred by darkness and the dizzying array of moving feet.

I keep glancing up, expecting to have lost Jeff, but he is head and shoulders above the crowd and easy to spot. And he's waiting for me, for Laney and Ed. Our small group sticks together.

Somewhere along the way, we lose Kim, Lori and gang. The four of us decide to grab an outside table at Shelby's Coffee Shop. Jeff asks for my order. When I try to give him money, he waves it off. "I've got it," he says. It feels different than a friend getting me coffee because I'm in a wheelchair and it's a pain to wait in line, let alone carry a drink. This feels chivalrous.

Jeff and Ed head inside to wait in line. Laney raises her eyebrows at me and grins, but says nothing. We wait for the men to return.

I wouldn't say I'm physically attracted to Jeff, but I'm not unattracted to him, either. I think about my silly crush on J.P., the ski instructor, and how pointless it was. This could have a point.

Now I'm fishing in my own pond. Crushing on my physical equivalent. Things have drastically changed for me. Why would I expect my relationships to be any different? Of course they don't work the same way. Lust doesn't come first anymore. Maybe that's a good thing.

We drink our coffee. The evening ends when Jeff looks at his watch and states the time. It's well past nine.

Jeff walks to his car, and Laney and Ed follow me home through residential streets. The headlights of Ed's car illuminate my way and allow other traffic to see me in my power chair much better than the pathetic flashlight I have gripped between my knees.

Laney leans out the open window to holler that I'm never doing this again and ask if my mother knows where I am and what I'm doing right now. The answer is no. She doesn't.

By the next morning, I'm talking sense to myself. I gave up dating a long time ago. What was I thinking? And Jeff isn't my physical equivalent. He walks. And when he looks at you, he's looking *right* at you. No confusion. Not to mention he drives, doesn't have to drink through a straw and doesn't need his mommy to cut his meat. Physical equivalent. Yeah, right. One too many glasses of wine is more like it.

That afternoon the phone rings. I pick it up.

"Hello, Amy?"

I recognize the garbled male voice on the other end right away. "Hi, Jeff."

Epilogue

THE SAME

A former coworker once set me up with someone I dated for a while. She told me, long after we'd broken up, he asked, "Will she ever be the same?" It's taken me years to be able to answer that question. It's been bouncing around my psyche ever since I heard it. I can answer it now.

I can't believe the things I was willing to do then, the people I was willing to reconnect with. Like that New Year's Eve I went out. As if nothing had changed. When everything had. I must not have known it or accepted it yet. I was still the old me in my head. I just hadn't caught my reflection in enough mirrors. Or seen the pitying looks on enough faces to bring about a realization. Now I steel myself against such looks. I avoid crowds instead of sashaying through them.

I know better now than to say yes to an old coworker who wants to see me. She did what was expected. A former colleague ends up in the hospital, you visit her at some point, right? People don't realize how life-altering the stroke was, how uncomfortable they'll be. What do you say in this situation? I'm sorry? What do you talk about? Office gossip seems extra meaningless.

Thank goodness I had some boundaries in place when old high school friends I hadn't seen in 20 years wanted to visit last year. I simply said, "No. I don't think it would be a good idea." I left it at that. It would be like showing up in my wheelchair to my high school reunion. Everyone goes to those things to show how well they're doing. Don't they? And there I'd be. It'd be a shock and a downer to everyone. All the balding men would breathe a sigh of relief. No way. No thanks.

But Val got to me early. I didn't know any better. I said yes. To make matters worse, my mother was still in denial herself. Why else would she suggest Valerie help me up the stairs? And why did I go along with the idea? Mom lived on the second floor then. I lived downstairs. My mother always wanted to show off her space, so she said she and Valerie could walk me up the stairs. No big deal. Yeah, right. When we reached the top, I was safely returned to my wheelchair, winded and shaking, Valerie dripped sweat.

I can't remember if the question was posed before or after that visit. Either way, I'm sure the episode was relayed to the ex, along with a resounding no, she won't *ever* be the same. Valerie never recovered either. I didn't hear from her again after that.

My own answer to the question is partly yes, mostly no. It depends on what he meant. I will guess he meant physically. Physically, no. I will never be the same again. I might always be in a wheelchair. Unless he believes in miracles. And I don't know if he does or not. How funny it is that I don't know that. He and I spent a long enough time together, but we didn't talk that way -- deep.

I believe in miracles. Small ones. Like the tight curl of a baby's fingers around one of your own. Or the soulful, brown eyes of a dog who looks deep into your eyes when you cry, gently licks your hand

and curls up next to you. Not the big miracles like walking on water, but the small fact that the clownfish is immune to the sting of the anemone. They need each other. That's a miracle. And elderly couples who die together. That's a miracle, too.

I believe things happen for a reason. If I'm supposed to be in a chair, I can't spend my life fighting to get out of it. This is my journey.

So no, physically, I won't ever be the same. Even if I can walk someday, I still have this voice. This hand. These eyes. I am forever changed.

But in another way, I've never changed. Except for maybe that first year -- when I say I wasn't myself, I have always been me. My personality is still the same. I'm grateful for that. I could have lost my language, my memories, my sense of humor. These are the things that really make me *me*. How does someone proceed to make a future without a past? My mom always jokes she'd have put me in a home if I didn't have my mind. She says she's kidding, but I wonder. And would I blame her? Then again, I've met the mother of a severely mentally challenged child, and she seemed as if she would fight forever. The maternal bond is like steel.

And again I'm back to being forever changed. And not just physically. Just as my memory of falling out of a treehouse when I was eight makes me who I am, this journey has shaped me. I've gained a whole new life experience, new perspective filled with a deeper compassion for my fellow human being. I've fully stepped into my own as a writer. I've experienced a renewed and richer relationship with my mother. I've gone from seeing her three times a year to talking to her every day. She knows what kind of toothpaste to buy, and how I like my oatmeal.

So that's the real question. "Would you trade all that to walk again? To walk and talk and look the same as you did before?"

And my answer is no. I wouldn't trade anything and I'll never be the same. Hey, the view from down here looks pretty good. Once you get past all the butts.

HOW TO HAVE YOUR OWN MISADVENTURES

1. ***Don't take things so seriously. Cultivate your sense of humor.***

   Learn to laugh at yourself. I don't mean to sound like an R.E.M. song, but it's a fact. People like to be around (and help) happy, smiling people. And let's face it, sometimes the most humorous thing about the situation is you…if you choose to see it. You may already stick out like a sore thumb and everybody's staring anyway - have some fun with it. It may be cliché, but laughter really is the best medicine.

2. ***Don't define yourself by tragedy.***

   Don't become known as "the girl in the wheelchair" or "the guy who had the skiing accident." Make your life about something more than whatever tragic thing happened to you. Do you want to be introduced as "the divorcée" forever? Make your story about something positive, not negative. There's power in words. If you're constantly reliving a negative event, through words or thoughts, you're putting that energy out into the world. Put positive out and get positive back.

3. *Consider getting a dog.*

I highly recommend living with an animal of some kind. It keeps you from getting lonely (if you live alone). One study showed that not only were pet owners less lonely, but they were healthier and had higher self-esteem too! Plus, owning a dog gets you outside for all those walks, rain or shine. And if you have a disability, a dog can be a great icebreaker. Many able-bodied people may stop to talk with you that normally would not have, which helps to build disability awareness. And there are so many homeless pets. Contact your local humane society, ASPCA or The National Association of Service Dogs.

4. *Live in a walkable community.*

If you can no longer drive, this is key to regaining your independence. Even if you still drive, life is too short to spend stressful hours in traffic. Getting out to grocery shop or run errands is good for you and allows you to meet your neighbors. And, if disabled, doing things for yourself can make you feel competent and confident!

5. *Get involved. Socialize. Help others.*

For me, all three of these things came together in Adaptive Sports and Recreation. Exercise is important for your physical and mental health. And most importantly, it allows you to make friends, often with people going through something similar. Call around. Your local hospital, rehab center or doctor's office may be a good place to start. Seek out support groups. You'll find there's usually always someone worse off than you. Offer your assistance or be a mentor to others. You'll find this gets you out of yourself and your own problems and reminds you to be grateful for what you have.

ABOUT THE AUTHOR

Amy Quincy earned a B.A. in English with a creative writing emphasis from Florida State University in 1992. She worked in several different corporate positions, became a massage therapist and built her own practice until 2006, when a stroke forced her to do something she now says she should have done a long time ago— commit to working full time on her writing. Amy has been published in *Skirt!, Talking Writing, Fiction Fix, Kaleidoscope, People of Few Words, Sasee Magazine* and has been featured in *The Florida Times-Union* and interviewed for The Badass Project.

Amy lives in Jacksonville, Florida with Bella, a persnickety kitty and Frankie, a Pekingese who monopolizes her time and is always up for a walk. Visit Amy at www.amyfquincy.wordpress.com.